Gotta Serve Somebody

Also by Graeme Carlé and published by
Emmaus Road Publishing

Eating Sacred Cows
A Closer Look at Tithing

Because of the Angels
Unveiling 1 Corinthians 11:2-16

The Red Heifer's Ashes
Mysteries of Ancient Israel

Born of the Spirit
A study guide for new believers

The Revelation series:
1. Dancing in the Dragon's Jaws
The Mystery of Israel's Survival

2. Slouching Towards Bethllehem
The Rise of the Antrichrists

3. Gotta Serve Somebody
The Mystery of the Marks & 666

4. Silencing the Witnesses
Jerusalem and The Ascent of Secularism

Gotta Serve Somebody

The Mystery of the Marks & 666

Graeme Carlé

© 2014 Graeme Carlé

First published 2014, revised 2018, 2020
Book design and production by Peter Aranyi
Cover design by Richard Westmoreland

ISBN 978-0-9582746-9-2

2020-41

Emmaus Road Publishing
PO Box 38 823 Howick, Auckland 2014 New Zealand
www.emmausroad.org.nz

Contents

Thanks

Again, to many friends for their love, support and feedback, especially Arthur Amon, Barbie & George Pauly, Benjamin & Dolly Pan, Chris Pan, Chris & Melissa Hennessy, Dave & Anneliesje Dobbyn, David Eves, David & Louise Lee, Deane McCracken, Elizabeth Rowe, Errol Francis, Kristin Herman, Marie Shaw, Olivia Ladyman, Peter Maddison, Peter & Miriam Woolston, Peter & Susan Ridley, Richard Westmoreland, Rory Cavanagh, Ross & Jenny Shaw, Steve & Simone Varney and Tom Gillooly. As for Peter Aranyi, how many lunches do I owe you now? I simply couldn't have done it without you.

Foreword

666. The mark of the beast. Or 'the number of his name' (Rev 13:17), or 'the number of the beast' (Rev 13:18).

For decades, rock musicians such as Black Sabbath, Iron Maiden, Led Zeppelin and Marilyn Manson have tried to shock us all by willingly accepting this number, featuring it on their album covers and T shirts or tattooing it on their bodies. While they have attracted the desired attention, it is clear they have no idea of its meaning.

There are *a number of ways* 666 can be understood.

If I was to ask you what exactly that *number of ways* is, i.e. how many ways can 666 be understood, your answer would not, of course, be a particular number, because 'a number of' is not literal but idiomatic. It actually means there are several options. Similarly, if we say there are *any number* of ways in which 666 can be understood, we are not being literal – 'any number' is a hyperbole, meaning 'a large and unlimited quantity'.[1]

We need to tread carefully with the numbers in Revelation 13:17-18 because numbering can be ambiguous and whenever we choose the wrong meaning, like a misread map, it leads us into a dead end. If, however, we turn back and choose the correct meaning, we can make good progress.

As for marks, what if you were to accept the warning of Charles Finney 'to mark the man who slanders everyone… and avoid him like you would a viper'? Good advice, but how exactly would you mark that one man? With a marker pen? And is there more than one to watch?

Or if we entertain Aristotle's axiom, 'it is the mark of an educated mind to be able to entertain a thought without accepting it', what kind of mark should we look for and where

---

1 www.thefreedictionary.com/number, 22 Nov, 2011.

---

exactly? On that person's forehead?

We see then that 'marks' too are ambiguous, and for too long we, scholars and lay people alike, have been careless in our exegesis of Revelation 13:16-18. There really are *a number* of ways this text can be read, the usual way today *marked* by the fear of a coming one-world monetary system which may never arrive. I believe the Lord will come before it does, and many Christians will find they have been like commuters waiting on the wrong platform for the train to pull in.

As well as Revelation 13:16-18, this book will also cover most of chapter 14, to see what happens to those who accept the mark of the beast, right up to the end of the harvest of the earth (v. 16). For any who may not know, these chapter and verse numbers in our Bibles today are a fairly recent addition to the original Hebrew and Greek texts, having been inserted in the 13th Century. While very helpful to navigate our way around the longer books, these breaks in the text can at times cause us to stop in the wrong place. Accordingly, we are going to ignore the break between chapters 13 and 14 because in the very first verse of chapter 14, which begins, 'And I saw…', John sees an amazing contrast between the mark of the beast and *the mark of God's name* being written on peoples' foreheads. We will therefore consider both of these marks.

Lastly, as in Books 1 and 2 in this series, in everything we consider, my assumption will be that it was readily understood by John's original hearers at the end of the 1st Century. Remember what the angel told Daniel in about 550 B.C:

> 8. As for me, I heard but could not understand; so I said, "My lord, what will be the outcome of these events?"
> 9. He said, "Go your way, Daniel, for these words are concealed and sealed up until the end time" (Dan 12:8-9)

Daniel's prophecies therefore were not to be understood in his time. Contrast that now with what the angel told John in about 95 A.D.:

And he said to me, "Do not seal up the words of the prophecy of this book, for the time is near" (Rev 22:10)

The Book of Revelation was an open book in the 1st Century. Accordingly, as you will see, the interpretation we will now establish in this book would have been available to any believer in John's audience who had been taught by the Twelve (Acts 2:42), or by those taught by them.

Introduction and Texts

Book 1

In our first study on Revelation's chapter 12, *Dancing in the Dragon's Jaws*, we saw that the woman is the nation of Israel 'according to the flesh', fulfilling God's plan to bring forth Messiah, His Son in flesh and blood. She did this despite the dragon's six genocidal attempts to thwart the plan, using the six great Gentile empires that had dominated or invaded Israel over her first two thousand years of history.

Tragically, as we saw, Israel as a nation then rejected her own Son, Jesus of Nazareth. As a direct consequence, they lost their land, their magnificent temple and their holy city, Jerusalem. However, God always remains faithful, not revoking His calling of her or reclaiming His gifts (Rom 11:29) which include the Promised Land, so her loss was not permanent but only for a time. She was sent back into 'the wilderness' where she was 'nourished' (vv. 6 and 14). This wilderness was not literally Sinai and Arabia but the metaphorical 'wilderness of the nations', i.e. the Gentiles (Ezek 20:35-36).[2]

Her time there is described as the mysterious time period of '1260 days' (v. 6) and 'a time and times and half a time' (v. 14), i.e. three and a half years. We were able to identify this, from Daniel's 70th week and Elijah's drought, as Jesus' "times of the Gentiles" (Luke 21:24). At this point, we were able to match this metaphorical time with real time, because Jesus said in 30 A.D. that it was to end with Israel regaining Jerusalem from the Gentiles. That is also now a matter of

---

2 Ezekiel's original audience clearly understood the metaphor some five hundred years before Christ. John's new reference to it is a repetition of the type or pattern in what is today often referred to as a prophetic recapitulation.

history – Israel regained Jerusalem in June 1967, for the first time in almost 2,000 years.[3]

Accordingly, we were able to establish that, like the woman and the seven-headed dragon, this time period is not literal but metaphorical. We concluded that the vision of Revelation 12 was to reveal some of the greatest mysteries of the Bible: *God's on-going plan for Israel; Israel's survival over the last 4,000 years,* despite Satan's genocidal attacks, and despite her rejection of Jesus of Nazareth in 30 A.D.; and the phenomenon of *ever-recurring anti-Semitism.*

The last verse of that chapter told us that when the dragon failed to prevent Messiah's coming and His resurrection, he turned to attack 'the rest of her offspring' (v. 17), i.e. every follower of the Messiah, whether Jew or Gentile.

Book 2

In our second study, *Slouching Towards Bethlehem,* which examined chapter 13:1-15, we saw details of that attack: how the dragon uses two zoomorphic entities, i.e. two spiritual beings which are portrayed as wild animals. The first beast we identified as the State going feral, when it abandons its God-given mandate to uphold justice and public order to become itself a god to be worshipped. The second beast, which looks like a lamb but speaks with the voice of a dragon, we found is the spirit of antichrist. This spirit causes 'those who dwell on the earth' (v. 14) to worship the first beast and its living image, which is its Head of State. In John's day, this worship was epitomised in the shrine at Pergamum dedicated to *Dea Roma et Augustus* or, in other words, the Goddess who is Rome and her emperor, Augustus Caesar.

---

3 They immediately handed back the heart of Jerusalem, the Temple Mount, to the Islamic authorities or empire so we cannot be too dogmatic about exact times here. While Israel has sovereignty, the times of the Gentiles may still not be complete until Israel also occupies the Temple Mount.

We saw how emperor-worship has occurred throughout the last 2,000 years. In the last one hundred years, this manifested around Stalin, Mussolini, Hirohito, Hitler, Mao Zedong, Pol Pot et al, but today it is primarily around Muhammad.

As to why this is allowed to happen, we saw that while the dragon gives the beasts his authority, ultimately it is God who allows them to function. Even though they blaspheme 'His name and His tabernacle, that is, those who dwell in heaven' (v. 6), it is God who gives the first beast the right 'to wage war with the saints and to overcome them' (v. 7). The vision of Revelation 13, therefore, explains another of the great mysteries of the Bible: *why, and for how long, does God allow the persecution and martyrdom of His people?*

We see again the mysterious time period – He will let these beasts act for 'forty-two months' (v. 5), the time that Israel, the woman, was to be in the wilderness. He is patiently waiting until the end of 'the partial hardening of Israel' (Rom 11:25) and of the times of the Gentiles which have extended from the 1st Century A.D. right up to our times.

Finally, we saw that in the 20th Century alone, the god-emperors have killed over 269 million men, women and children who have resisted them or got in their way.

Book 3

We have now come to the last three verses of Revelation 13 which describe the infamous mark of the first beast and the number of his name. Since these beasts have been operating throughout the last two thousand years, so too has the mark, contrary to much of what is thought and taught today, which has most of Revelation applying only to a future time called The Great Tribulation.

See for example the Christian publishing phenomenon of Tim LaHaye and Jerry Jenkins' *Left Behind* series, which sold more than 65 million books and sparked three action thriller movies; computer games, radio dramas, audio CDs and teenage versions.[4] In these books, the first beast is not the geo-political state which we established in Book 2 but a future tyrannical individual and his mark is an implanted microchip.

We, however, will read on into chapter 14, to see more of the immediate context before considering the bigger picture of the entire Old and New Testaments' use of marks, signs and seals.

You will then be able to see for yourself how the mark of the beast is not a future event based around our shopping. It was prefigured in Exodus chapter 13 in about 1500 B.C. and actually observed by John and his audience in the 1st Century A.D. Accordingly, instead of waiting for it to happen, we should be recognising it occurring virtually before our eyes today.

We need to pray again:

> Open my eyes, that I may behold wonderful things from Your law;
> I am a stranger in the earth; do not hide Your commandments from me (Psa 119:18-19)

Revelation 13

> 16. And he causes all, the small and the great, and the rich and the poor, and the free men and the slaves, to be given a mark on their right hand, or on their forehead,
> 17. and he provides that no one should be able to buy or sell, except the one who has the mark, either the name of the beast or the number of his name.
> 18. Here is wisdom. Let him who has understanding calculate the number of the beast, for the number is that of a man; and his number is six hundred and sixty-six.

---

4 The sixteen novels, published between 1995 and 2007, were followed by *Left Behind: The Kids*, forty more novels for teenagers and young adults, co-written with Chris Fabry between 1998 and 2004. Available in 12 languages, they are now being prepared in another 16. Tyndale House Publishers, www.leftbehind.com, 26 Aug, 2011.

Revelation 14

1. Then I looked, and behold, the Lamb was standing on Mount Zion, and with Him one hundred and forty-four thousand, having His name and the name of His Father written on their foreheads.

2. And I heard a voice from heaven, like the sound of many waters and like the sound of loud thunder, and the voice which I heard was like the sound of harpists playing on their harps.

3. And they sang a new song before the throne and before the four living creatures and the elders; and no one could learn the song except the one hundred and forty-four thousand who had been purchased from the earth.

4. These are the ones who have not been defiled with women, for they have kept themselves chaste. These are the ones who follow the Lamb wherever He goes. These have been purchased from among men as first fruits to God and to the Lamb.

5. And no lie was found in their mouth; they are blameless.

6. And I saw another angel flying in midheaven, having an eternal gospel to preach to those who live on the earth, and to every nation and tribe and tongue and people;

7. and he said with a loud voice, "Fear God, and give Him glory, because the hour of His judgment has come; worship Him who made the heaven and the earth and sea and springs of waters."

8. And another angel, a second one, followed, saying, "Fallen, fallen is Babylon the great, she who has made all the nations drink of the wine of the passion of her immorality."

9. Then another angel, a third one, followed them, saying with a loud voice, "If anyone worships the beast and his image, and receives a mark on his forehead or on his hand,

10. he also will drink of the wine of the wrath of God, which is mixed in full strength in the cup of His anger; and he will be tormented with fire and brimstone in the presence of the holy angels and in the presence of the Lamb.

11. "And the smoke of their torment goes up forever and ever; they have no rest day and night, those who worship the beast and his image, and whoever receives the mark of his name."

12. Here is the perseverance of the saints who keep the commandments of God and their faith in Jesus.

Gotta Serve Somebody

13. And I heard a voice from heaven, saying, "Write, 'Blessed are the dead who die in the Lord from now on!'""Yes," says the Spirit, "so that they may rest from their labors, for their deeds follow with them."

14. Then I looked, and behold, a white cloud, and sitting on the cloud was one like a son of man, having a golden crown on His head and a sharp sickle in His hand.

15. And another angel came out of the temple, crying out with a loud voice to Him who sat on the cloud, "Put in your sickle and reap, for the hour to reap has come, because the harvest of the earth is ripe."

1

20th Century Thinking
Predicted Technology?

The *Left Behind* novels by Christian writers Tim LaHaye and Jerry Jenkins[5] well illustrate the most popular understanding of the mark in American Christian thinking today. In book eight, *The Mark: the Beast Rules the World,* one of the fictional characters explains how their idea of the mark works:

> "The first page of your folders… is a listing of the ten world regions and a corresponding number. It is the product of a mathematical equation that identifies those regions and their relationships to His Excellency the Potentate [the AntiChrist, named Nicolae Jetty Carpathia]. The loyalty mark… shall begin with these numbers, thus identifying the home region of every citizen. The subsequent numbers, embedded on a biochip inserted under the skin, will further identify the person to the point where every one shall be unique…The mark shall consist of the name of His Excellency or the prescribed number"…

> "We have settled on the technology", Viv continued. "The miniature biochip with the suffix numbers embedded in it can be inserted as painlessly as a vaccination in a matter of seconds. Citizens may chose either location, and visible will be a thin, half-inch scar, and to its immediate left, in six-point black ink -impossible to remove under penalty of law – the number that designates the home region of the individual. That number may be included in the embedded chip, should the person prefer that one of the variations of the name of the potentate appear on their flesh".

---

5 Tyndale House Publishers.

Gotta Serve Somebody

"Variations?" someone asked.

"Yes. Most, we assume, will prefer the understated numbers next to the thin scar. But they may also choose from the small initials – no bigger than the numbers – NJC – the first or last name may be used, including one version of Nicolae that would virtually cover the left side of the forehead".6

Later, another character describes the choice offered citizens:

"In a few moments you will be led to the central building, where you will tell the staff whether you want your loyalty mark on your forehead or your right hand. The area you choose will then be disinfected with an alcohol solution. When it is your turn, you will enter a cubicle, where you will sit and be injected with a biochip, while simultaneously tattooed with the prefix 216, which identifies you as a citizen of the United Carpathian States. The application takes just seconds."7

In these novels, anyone accepting the biochip will then be able to "buy or sell". But what of the far more horrifying consequences described in the Scriptures we have just read in Revelation 14?

9. Then another angel, a third one, followed them, saying with a loud voice, "If anyone worships the beast and his image, and receives a mark on his forehead or on his hand,
10. he also will drink of the wine of the wrath of God, which is mixed in full strength in the cup of His anger; and he will be tormented with fire and brimstone in the presence of the holy angels and in the presence of the Lamb.
11. "And the smoke of their torment goes up forever and ever; they have no rest day and night, those who worship the beast and his image, and whoever receives the mark of his name" (Rev 14:9-11)

---

6 Tim LaHaye and Jerry Jenkins, *The Mark: The Beast Rules the World*, Tyndale House Publishers, 2000, pp. 85-86.
7 Ibid., p. 285.

According to John, the mark is the basis for God's judgement. In order to explain their interpretation, Tim LaHaye and Jerry Jenkins have also written in non-fictional form:

> Concerned believers sometimes worry that they might somehow inadvertently receive this devilish mark. But this is impossible. First, we should remember that our God is loving and merciful; He proved that forever in the gift of His Son. We should see Him as our heavenly Father who stands at the gate of heaven, letting men and women into His paradise, not trying to keep them out. It would be totally out of character for Him to send someone to hell for accidently standing in the wrong line and getting the mark of the Beast, when he really wanted the mark of the Father. Second, the aforementioned verses show that the mark is obtained only by those who sell their soul to the Beast and the devil who gives him his power. This involves a willful rejection of God – something a true Christian could never do.[8]

They therefore include in the ninth book one character, Chang Wong, who receives the mark of the beast but is not condemned by God since it was implanted in him after he had been drugged by his father so he was not personally "worshipping the beast and his image" when he received it.

The Last 100 Years

Over the last one hundred years there have been many other widely-published interpretations which seek to match the technology of the day.

In 1918, long before biochips, the author of the famous *Bible Prophecy Charts*, Clarence Larkin, wrote:

> The "Mark" will be branded or burnt on. It will probably be the "number of the beast" or "666".[9]

---

8 Tim LaHaye and Jerry Jenkins, *Are We Living in the End Times?* Tyndale House, 1999, pp. 196-197.
9 Clarence Larkin, *Dispensational Truth*, 1918, p. 124.

                                          Gotta Serve Somebody

In 1946, M.R. DeHaan noted his contemporaries liking tattoos so:

> There are many who believe that the mark will consist of the number 666 tattooed upon the foreheads and hands of the followers of the beast.[10]

In 1973, the introduction of UPC (Universal Product Code) barcodes created another possible fulfilment. Revolutionising shopping, this mark is now on virtually everything sold in shops in the Western world. Although only on the products so far and not containing much information, would this be adapted to the people buying them?

However, by 1978, ultra-violet light and laser technology seemed more probable to Salem Kirban in *Satan's Mark Exposed*:

> The Mark will be a "harmless" and "invisible" Laser Beam applied mark. You will have the choice of having the Mark placed on your right hand or on your forehead! [11]

> What this identifying mark will be… the Lord has not desired to make clear to us at this time. Nor can we know at this time the identity of Antichrist. It may be the number "666" which is the number of man…[12]

> What will be his mark?… It appears that it will be some sort of credit card number and loyalty badge combined into one. Possibly it may be a tattoo invisible to the naked eye but visible upon some type of light-beam scan. It will, however, in its numerical aspect have some logo type connection with the number 666, or a code based on these digits, which will be related directly to the name of the Antichrist.[13]

---

10   M.R. DeHaan, *Studies in Revelation*, 1946, p. 188.
11   Salem Kirban, *Satan's Mark Exposed*, 1978, p. 99.
12   Ibid., p. 123.
13   Dr. Gary G. Cohen, cited by Salem Kirban, Ibid., p. 131.

Before the *Left Behind* series, the most popular Christian exposition of these verses was *The Late, Great Planet Earth* by Hal Lindsey and Carole C. Carlson. It sold *over 35 million copies* in the 1970s and was translated into more than fifty languages. In a follow-up, *The 1980's: Countdown to Armageddon,* Mr Lindsey wrote:

> Those worshippers will each be assigned a trade number. Without that number, no one will be permitted to buy or sell anything… The only safeguard would be to tattoo the number on your skin with an ink that could be seen only in a special light… The anti-Christ, with the help of his false prophet, will require that a number representing his name become part of your own banking number to make it valid.[14]

In the 1990s, Dave Hunt saw a microchip as more probable:

> A tiny computer chip painlessly and quickly implanted just under the skin in hand or forehead will likely become the means of fulfilling this prophecy.[15]

So too did Terry Cook in *The Mark of the New World Order:*

> It is my well-researched opinion that the Mark of the Beast, as related in Scripture, is absolutely literal. Soon, all people on earth will be coerced into accepting a mark in their right hand or forehead. I am convinced that it will be an injectable passive RFID transponder with a computer chip – a literal injection with a literal electronic biochip 'mark'… I believe that such an implanted identification mark literally will become Satan's Mark of the Beast.[16]

Others were not so convinced.

M.R. DeHaan wrote of his doubts in 1946:

---

14   Hal Lindsey and Carole C. Carlson, *The 1980's: Countdown to Armageddon,* 1980, pp. 110-112.
15   Dave Hunt, *How Close Are We?* 1993, p. 261
16   Terry Cook, *The Mark of the New World Order,* 1996, p. 587.

Gotta Serve Somebody

What this mark of the beast will be we may not know
now. Hundreds of answers have been suggested, but I
do not believe these are scriptural. Men have tried to
identify this Antichrist, and there have been hundreds of
guesses concerning his identity, but all of them have been
wrong... It is foolish, therefore, to speculate concerning
his identity. The same is true of the mark of the beast.
What the mark will be we do not know.[17]

J. Dwight Pentecost likewise in 1961:

I confess that I don't know what this number means.
I am certain, however, that there are more than 666
interpretations. Everyone seems to have an opinion. Since
God doesn't explain the meaning, apparently it's not
important for us to know. Before this person comes to
prominence believers will have been translated into God's
presence. We will not have the slightest interest in the
Beast or the False Prophet because we will be occupied
with the Lord Jesus Christ in glory. The reason God gave
us any information at all, I believe, is so that believers alive
in that day will have a clear identifying sign that the one
in world power is Satan's masterpiece.[18]

Literal or Metaphorical?

Then there are those who see the mark and the number as
metaphorical. In 1939, William Hendriksen wrote:

These theories err in... that they interpret the mark as a
single, individual, outward, visible sign... Receiving the
mark of the beast on the forehead or right hand indicates
that the person so characterized belongs to the company
of those who persecute the Church; and that – either
preeminently in what he thinks, says, writes or more
emphatically in what he does – this antichristian spirit
becomes evident...

---

17 M.R. DeHaan, *Studies in Revelation*, 1946, pp. 187-188.
18 J. Dwight Pentecost, *Prophecy for Today*, 1961, p. 114.

> Six… is not seven and never reaches seven. It always fails
> to attain to perfection; that is, it never becomes seven.
> Six means missing the mark, or failure. Seven means
> perfection or victory… The number of the beast is 666,
> that is, failure upon failure upon failure! It is the number
> of man, for the beast glories in man; and must fail![19]

Others see the mark as literal but the number as metaphorical.
N.T. Wright, for example, places the mark in the 1st Century
as:

> …a formal requirement that unless you had offered the
> required sacrifices [to Caesar] you weren't allowed in the
> market. There were various kinds of marks and visible
> signs which were used to set people apart either as 'able to
> trade' or as 'not able to trade'…

> It is more or less certain that the number 666 represents,
> by one of many formulae well known at the time,
> the name NERO CAESAR when written in Hebrew
> characters… The monster who was, is not, and is to come
> looks pretty certainly to be Nero.

> But the number 666 isn't just a cryptogram. It's also a
> parody. The number of perfection, not least for John,
> would be, we assume, 777. Some have even suggested that
> the name JESUS comes out, in some systems, as 888 – a
> kind of super-perfection. But for John there is little doubt.
> Nero, and the system he represented and embodied, was
> but a parody of the real thing, one short of the right
> number three times over. Jesus was the reality; Nero, just a
> dangerous, blasphemous copy.[20]

---

19 William Hendriksen, *More Than Conquerors*, Grand Rapids; Baker
Book House, 1986, pp. 150-151.
20 N.T. Wright, *Revelation For Everyone*, London; SPCK, 2011, pp.
121-122.

                                          Gotta Serve Somebody

2nd Century Thinking

Eighteen hundred years earlier, in about 170-180 A.D., Irenaeus (ca. 130-202 A.D.) wrote his best guess:

> Then also Lateinos has the number six hundred and sixty-six; and it is a very probable [solution], this being the name of the last kingdom [of the four seen by Daniel]. For the Latins [i.e. Romans] are they who at present bear rule: I will not, however, make any boast over this [coincidence].[21]

Latin, Greek and Hebrew are alphanumeric languages, i.e. some of their alphabet letters have numeric equivalent, as we still use today in Latin or Roman numerals, I, V, X, L, C, D, M (i.e. 1, 5, 10, 50, 100, 500, 1000). Irenaeus saw that *Lateinos,* Greek for "the Latin speaking man", adds up to 666 as follows:

L (lambda) =	30
A (alpha) =	1
T (tau) =	300
E (epsilon) =	5
I (iota) =	10
N (nu) =	50
O (omicron) =	70
S (sigma) =	200
	666

Figure (i) 'Calculating' the number

Not only was Irenaeus not confident, he warned against 'counting the number of the beast':

> It is therefore more certain, and less hazardous, to await the fulfillment of the prophecy, than to be making

---

21 Irenaeus of Lyons, *Against Heresies*, Book 5, chapter 30, para 3.

surmises, and casting about for any names that may present themselves, inasmuch as *many names can be found* possessing the number mentioned; and the same question will, after all, remain unsolved. For if there are many names found possessing this number, it will be asked which among them shall the coming man bear? [22]

Another Way Forward

Irenaeus's conclusion is, of course, perfectly correct and applies to ever more possibilities today. Fortunately, there is another way of interpreting these verses which does not require any 'counting the number' or pointless 'surmises' regarding the 'many names possessing the number'. Nor does it require trying to figure out which particular 21st Century technology John might mean.

Let us simply do as we have done so far – focus on all of John's phrases and symbols in the light of both the Old Testament's use of those and the New Testament's inspired commentary on them. Here is our text again:

> 16. And he causes all, the small and the great, and the rich and the poor, and the free men and the slaves, to be given a mark on their right hand, or on their forehead,
> 17. and he provides that no one should be able to buy or to sell, except the one who has the mark, either the name of the beast or the number of his name.
> 18. Here is wisdom. Let him who has understanding, calculate the number of the beast, for the number is that of a man; and his number is six hundred and sixty-six.

Who is 'he' (v. 16)? From verses 11-15, 'he' is the second beast, which is the spirit of antichrist, as we established in Book 2.[23] This spirit causes all to be marked with 'the name of the beast or the number of his name' (v. 17). Which beast's name

---

22   Ibid., emphasis added.
23   *Slouching Towards Bethlehem (the Rise of the Antichrists).*

                    Gotta Serve Somebody

or number? From verses 14-15, the first beast's, which we also established in Book 2 is the principality and power of the State. In other words, *the spirit of antichrist will cause all to be given the mark of the principality and power of the State.*

Who are actually given this mark? 'All, the small and the great, and the rich and the poor, and the free men and the slaves' (v. 16).

Or are they? Most reading this passage stop at v. 18 because it is the chapter end. However, as mentioned earlier, we need to read the next verse as well because these chapter numbers and verses are not part of the inspired text:

> And I looked, and behold, the Lamb was standing on Mount Zion, and with Him one hundred and forty-four thousand, having His name and the name of His Father written on their foreheads (Rev 14:1)

We see then that it is *not* everyone who is marked with the name or number of the beast as at least these 144,000 are not. Instead, they are marked with the name of the Lamb 'and the name of His Father… on their foreheads'. We will leave identifying the 144,000 until later. First, we need to understand both marks.

What the Mark of the Beast is *Not*

As we have seen, many have thought the mark of the beast will be both future and literal, whether branded, tattooed, barcoded, laser-beamed or micro-chipped onto peoples' foreheads or right hands, like the number the Nazis forced on the inmates of their concentration camps. Seeing its relevance to buying and selling, some equate it to the West's move towards a cashless society. To avoid disfiguring people, they say, the mark could be a permanent version of what Disneyland already uses, removable marks on the backs of customers' hands that only become visible under ultraviolet light. Others point to the newly developed use of identification micro-chips, installed in vehicles or surgically implanted just under the skin on prize animals.

This seems perfectly reasonable because plastic credit or debit cards can be replaced by any of this technology and the advantages are obvious – you cannot lose your identification and it cannot be easily stolen.

Studying this subject since 1973, I could not identify the fatal flaw in this interpretation of the mark of the beast until about 1985 when I was talking with a Christian friend who worked in a bank. He was both afraid and excited because, as he told me, he could see the financial technology was close to where it could be a logical step to give every child an identification number at birth. While still in the hospital, the baby could be issued his or her number with a minimum of fuss, in much the same way as vaccinations are done today.

As I listened, I suddenly *knew* this actually guaranteed it could not be the mark of the beast. I knew, not because of the huge outcry from civil rights groups, but on the basis of the same Scriptures that worry Tim LaHaye and Jerry Jenkins:

> If anyone worships the beast and his image, and receives a mark on his forehead or upon his hand, he also will drink of the wine of the wrath of God, which is mixed in full strength in the cup of his anger; and he will be tormented with fire and brimstone in the presence of the holy angels and in the presence of the Lamb.
> And the smoke of their torment goes up forever and ever; and they have no rest day and night, those who worship the beast and his image, or whoever who receives the mark of his name (Rev 14:9-11)

The consequence of bearing this mark is the loss of all hope. It is a means by which God determines who is saved and who is lost, 'forever and ever' (v. 11).[24] As I listened to my friend, I realised that if the mark of the beast could be simply

---

24 This torment is itself a huge and controversial subject and will be addressed in a later study on heaven and hell.

                                          Gotta Serve Somebody

applied to a baby at birth, a child at school, or a concentration camp inmate, then God would be condemning the victims, beyond all recourse, on the basis of someone else's choices and actions. This interpretation denigrates the character of God as a righteous judge. It also defies the plain teaching of many Scriptures, such as:

> The person who sins will die. The son will not bear the punishment for the father's iniquity, nor will the father bear the punishment for the son's iniquity… (Ezek 18:20)

The mark of the beast, as this book will demonstrate, is in fact:

(i) Not a **literal** mark, whether burnt, tattooed, lasered on or implanted in the right hand or forehead of anyone, new-born baby or adult.

(ii) Not **able to be imposed** on anyone except by their own choice to worship the beast or his image.

(iii) Not **permanent**. If it is, that would mean those receiving it are all reprobate, i.e. unable to repent. Biblically, this was a rare condition, as it is in our society today.

(iv) Not **yet to happen**. It has already manifested numerous times over the last two thousand years!

Our mistake is that we have been looking at the Book of Revelation through the wrong lenses, those of 21st Century Gentiles. We have looked at today's technology and then read into Revelation what we can achieve now. Instead, we should have been asking ourselves, what would the people to whom Revelation was actually written have heard? Remember, this was a letter written to seven churches in Asia Minor (Rev 1:4) two thousand years ago. What did 'a mark on their right hand or on their forehead' mean to these 1st Century Jews and their new Gentile friends?

It has taken me almost thirty years to finally, completely answer these questions and thus catch up to the starting point of the 1st Century saints. Hopefully, I can now explain it clearly and save you time.

2

The Marks of God
Bearing His Name

To understand the mark of the beast, we must first understand God's use of marks because, as we saw, there are two in our text: 'the name of the beast or the number of his name' (Rev 13:17) and 'the name of the Lamb and the name of His Father written on their foreheads' (Rev 14:1).

We also need to learn what Jesus and His 1st Century Jewish disciples would have already known – that God Himself began the whole system of *marking, numbering and putting His name* on people, in particular *on their foreheads and on their hands,* one and a half thousand years earlier.

When the extended family that was Israel left Egypt in the 15th Century B.C., God told them that He was placing a mark on their foreheads and hands, as recorded in the Book of Exodus, and then He numbered them. They had a whole book dedicated to this, the Book of Numbers, and today we seem to have completely overlooked its significance. These two books, therefore, can help us these thousands of years later to catch up with the 1st Century believers.

The mark of the beast is simply a corollary or demonic counterpart of that. As we now examine these actions of God, we will see how the spirit of antichrist imitates them, putting other names on people by marking and numbering them.

In ancient times, as it is today, the primary purpose of making a mark of your name was like a hand-written signature, to proclaim ownership or authenticity. For example, in about 60 A.D.

> I, Paul, write this greeting with my own hand, and this is a distinguishing mark in every letter; this is the way I write (2 Thess 3:17)

Sometimes it was in the form of a metal seal, a unique mark, pressed into clay, as in Job 38:14, or into wax on documents, as in King Ahasuerus's command to Mordecai in about 473 B.C.[25]:

> "Now you write to the Jews as you see fit, in the king's name, and seal it with the king's signet ring; for a decree which is written in the name of the king and sealed with the king's signet ring may not be revoked" (Est 8:8)

These seals were often worn on a cord around the neck for security (Gen 38:18, Song 8:6).

As we will see, neither the mark of God nor the mark of the beast was, or is, to give anyone access to a bank account, nor are they any form of personal or individual identification. Both marks signify *ownership and protection* – God looks after His people and, as they say, 'the devil looks after his own'. Both marks are voluntarily received and can be swapped at almost any time because they proclaim the *present status* of who belongs to whom.

Before we look at Exodus and Numbers, however, let us look at an overview of God's marks in the Old Testament.

Marks, Signs and Seals

Besides marks being impressed into wax or clay seals, some events and objects are also described as 'signs',[26] authenticating the hand of God in or on them. The Hebrew noun *oth* comes from a verb to mark or sign, and is used both literally and figuratively to denote a mark, sign, flag, beacon, monument or token,[27] and what we today call our *signature*.

Some are evidence of the power and/or character of God. For example, the stars are *oth* or signs (Gen 1:14), as are

---

25 Date according to *The Zondervan Pictorial Encyclopedia of the Bible,* Vol.2, p. 376.
26 The same Hebrew word, *oth*, is used; the distinction is usually made by English translators.
27 *NAS Exhaustive Concordance of the Bible*, p. 1486.

Gotta Serve Somebody

rainbows (Gen 9:12-17), the miracles performed by Moses for Pharaoh (Exo 4:8), His judgements (Deut 28:46), and reminders of those (Num 16:38, 17:10).

Two, particularly, required human cooperation: circumcision and Sabbath-keeping.

(i) Circumcision

God told Abraham, who was aged 99 at the time:

> "This is My covenant, which you shall keep, between Me and you and your descendants after you: every male among you shall be circumcised.
> "And you shall be circumcised in the flesh of your foreskin, and it shall be *the sign of the covenant* between Me and you"
> (Gen 17:10-11, emphasis added)

Abraham and his descendants needed to respond, to create this sign or mark in their flesh, to be in the covenant; any who did not create the sign were breaking it:

> "But an uncircumcised male who is not circumcised in the flesh of his foreskin, that person shall be cut off from his people; he has broken My covenant" (Gen 17:14)

Moses was severely rebuked by God and his wife Zipporah for failing to circumcise his son (Exo 4:24-26) and it became mandatory to circumcise baby boys on the eighth day (Lev 12:3). However, Israel as a nation was slow to learn and Joshua needed to re-establish it for the next generation after the forty years in the wilderness (Josh 5:2-9).

The interchangeability of marks or signs and seals can be seen in Paul's description of Abraham:

> ...he received the *sign* [Greek, *semeion*] of circumcision, a *seal* [Greek, *sphragis*] of the righteousness of the faith which he had while uncircumcised (Rom 4:11, emphasis added)

Obviously, this literal, physical sign of the Abrahamic and Mosaic Covenants was necessarily only on the males but God wanted both men and women to circumcise their hearts, to cut off any bad attitudes:

> "So circumcise your heart, and stiffen your neck no longer."
> (Deut 10:16)

> "Moreover the LORD your God will circumcise your heart and the heart of your descendants, to love the LORD your God with all your heart and with all your soul, so that you may live."
> (Deut 30:6)

In the New Covenant, physical circumcision is replaced by water baptism[28] for both male and female believers, where we are to become disciples and put off 'the body of the flesh' or carnal nature (Col 2:11-12, Rom 6:1-7). Since this is not achieved by water but by our free-will choices, baptism can only ever be an outward sign.

(ii) Sabbath-keeping

The Mosaic Covenant also required cooperation from all in Israel, both male and female, in the sign of the Sabbath:

> 13. "You shall surely observe My sabbaths; for this is *a sign* between Me and you throughout your generations, that you may know that I am the LORD who sanctifies you…
> 15. "For six days work may be done, but on the seventh day there is a sabbath of complete rest, holy to the LORD; whoever does any work on the sabbath day shall surely be put to death.
> 16. "So the sons of Israel shall observe the sabbath, to celebrate the sabbath throughout their generations as a perpetual covenant.'
> 17. "It is *a sign* between Me and the sons of Israel forever; for in six days the LORD made heaven and earth, but on the seventh day He ceased from labor, and was refreshed"
> (Ex 31:13-17, emphasis added)

---

28   In the 1st Century, water baptism was the usual way of personally committing to follow Christ, e.g. Mark 16:16, Acts 2:38, 1 Peter 3:21. However, it was not an essential ritual for salvation (Luke 23:42-43).

                                                  Gotta Serve Somebody

Notice, this sign was not a literal or visible mark but *metaphorical*: all in Israel who kept the seventh day Sabbath bore the 'sign' or mark of God; those who did not keep it, did not bear the mark.

It was recognising this that led Seventh Day Adventist leader and prophetess Ellen G. White to her conclusion that observing the Sabbath on Sunday is the mark of the beast:

> ...all we were required to do was to give up God's Sabbath, and keep the Pope's, and then we should have the mark of the Beast, and of his image.[29]

> ...worship the beast or his image by keeping the first day of the week. The observance of this day is the mark of the beast.[30]

She was heading in the right metaphorical direction but, as we will see, ended up in the wrong place. Her mistake came from misinterpreting the two beasts of Revelation 13, writing in *The Great Controversy* that the first beast is the Papacy[31] and the second beast is the United States of America.[32] Accordingly, she thought the image of the first beast...:

> ...represents that form of apostate Protestantism which will be developed when the Protestant churches shall seek the aid of the civil power for the enforcement of their dogmas... It will be only a step to the resort to force.[33]

In the New Covenant, however, it simply does not matter which day, if any, is observed because it is a matter of individual conscience:

---

29 *A Word to the "Little Flock"*, p. 19, 1847.

30 *Testimonies to Ministers and Gospel Workers*, p. 133, 1898. http://text.egwwritings.org/publication.php?pubtype=Book&bookCode=WLF&pagenumber=19 and ...Book&bookCode=TM&lang=en&pagenumber=133, 13 Feb, 2013.

31 *The Great Controversy (Between Christ and Satan)*, Mountain View; Pacific Press, Sixth Edition, 1974, p. 392. First published in 1911.

32 Ibid., p. 388.

33 Ibid., p. 392.

> One person regards one day above another, another regards
> every day alike. Each person must be fully convinced in his own
> mind (Rom 14:5)

This is because the Sabbath was a 'shadow', foreshadowing the relief we find in Jesus when we fully trust in His works instead of our own (Col 2:16-17). As the writer to the Hebrews puts it:

> 9. So there remains a Sabbath rest for the people of God.
> 10. For the one who has entered His rest has himself also rested
> from his works, as God did from His. (Heb 4:9-10)

These two cooperative signs, circumcision and Sabbath-keeping, therefore were to foreshadow New Covenant marks, signs or seals of God's ownership.

Paul used 'seal' as a metaphor for validation: the Corinthians were the seal of his apostleship (1 Cor 9:2); the Corinthians and the Ephesians were sealed with the Holy Spirit (2 Cor 1:22, Eph 1:13, 4:30); the church bears the seal of God's knowing them and their abstaining from evil (2 Tim 2:19).

John's Gospel likewise uses 'seal' as a metaphor: those who accept Jesus' testimony have added their own signature (John 3:33); the Father has 'set His seal' on the Son (John 6:27).

We see then that marks, signs and seals denote ownership or authenticity, and can be literal or metaphorical.

Let us now turn to marks said to be on particular individuals.

Cain's Mark

The first mention of a mark in the Scriptures is the infamous mark of Cain:

> So the LORD said to him [Cain], "Therefore whoever kills Cain,
> vengeance will be taken on him sevenfold". And the LORD
> appointed *a sign* for [KJV, set a mark on] Cain, lest anyone
> finding him should slay him. (Gen 4:15, emphasis added)

Cain had just killed Abel and was being sent into exile

Gotta Serve Somebody

(Gen 4:11-12). He is afraid that "whoever finds me will kill me" (v. 14), so God promises to *protect* him and marks him accordingly. As you can see, the text gives no description at all of the sign or mark but, historically, some have believed it was black skin, as in this ancient comment from 5th or 6th Century Armenia:

> And the Lord was wroth with Cain… He beat Cain's face with hail, which blackened like coal, and thus he remained with a black face.[34]

Tragically, in more recent times many in the southern United States also believed this. In 1773, America's first black woman poet and slave, Phillis Wheatley, wrote of this hateful prejudice but also of her own sure faith:

> 'Twas mercy brought me from my pagan land,
> Taught my benighted soul to understand
> That there's a God, that there's a Savior too:
> Once I redemption neither sought nor knew.
> Some view our sable race with scornful eye,
> "Their color is a diabolic dye".
> Remember Christians; Negroes, black as Cain,
> May be refin'd, and join th' angelic train.[35]

When the Southern Baptists split from the Northern Baptists over slavery and racial segregation, they used the curse and mark of Cain as their doctrinal justification, not officially repudiating it until 1995. The founding prophets of the Church of Jesus Christ of Latter Day Saints (aka Mormonism) taught similarly,[36] but their successors officially repudiated it in 1978.

---

34 William Lipscomb, *The Armenian Apocryphal Adam Literature,* Atlanta, Scholars Press, 1990 pp. 160 & 271.
35 Phillis Wheatley, *On Being Brought From Africa to America,* www.earlyamerica.com/review/winter96/wheatley.html, 29 May, 2009.
36 For example, Brigham Young in 1852: "What is that mark? You will see it on the countenance of every African you ever did see upon the face of the earth, or ever will see... I tell you, this people that are commonly called Negroes are the children of old Cain", Msd 1234, Box

Of course, Noah's flood ensured we are all descendants of the eight preserved on the ark so all skin colour variations come from them. We should therefore ignore Darwin's 'races', especially 'favoured races',[37] and speak instead of people-groups – there is only one race, the human race, to which we all belong.

What then was the mark on Cain?

As we saw above, the Hebrew noun *oth* means an ownership mark. The mark of Cain was *not* a badge of shame but of God's continuing grace and protection. As Ray C. Stedman wrote:

> God throws a circle of protective love about Cain and says, "Yes, he is guilty. He's a murderer - but he is still my property, and don't forget it in your dealings with him". Thus the mark of Cain is not a mark of shame, as we usually interpret it. It is not a mark to brand him in the eyes of others as a terrible murderer, to be shunned and treated as a pariah. It is rather, a mark of grace, by which God is saying, "This man is still my property. Hands off!" Thus the heart of God is always ready to show mercy. There can only be one reason why God thus protected Cain. It was in order to give him time to think and to repent. This is always the way of God. Peter says, in his second letter, "Do not ever make the mistake of regarding the longsuffering of God as weakness" (2 Pet 3:9).[38]

We are nowhere told how or where Cain was marked. Accordingly, while the mark could have been a visible mark on Cain's skin, that is unlikely because God later expressly

---

48, Folder 3, LDS Church Historical Dept.

37   Charles Darwin, *On the Origin of Species by Means of Natural Selection, or the Preservation of Favoured Races in the Struggle for Life,* 1859. Famed evolutionist Stephen Jay Gould was candid about this: 'Biological arguments for racism may have been common before 1859, but they increased by orders of magnitude following the acceptance of evolutionary theory.' S.J. Gould, *Ontogeny and Phylogeny,* Cambridge, Massachusetts; Belknap-Harvard Press, 1977, pp. 127-128.

38   www.pbc.org/files/messages/3394/0322.html, 28 May, 2009.

                    Gotta Serve Somebody

forbade tattooing:

> You shall not make any cuts in your body for the dead nor make any tattoo marks on yourselves: I am the LORD (Lev 19:28)

As we will see next, none of God's other marks were literal marks on skin so perhaps Cain's mark was a tangible sense of God's presence or hand upon him, or simply his reputation as noted by Lamech (Gen 4:24).

There is, however, no doubt as to its purpose: Cain wanted protection and this mark of God was to let everyone know that he was under God's protection; if they harmed him, God would punish them "sevenfold" (Gen 4:15).

Aaron's 'Name on His Forehead'

Much later, Aaron received a mark of God's ownership, not for protection but for identification. It was the name of the Lord on his forehead but it was not on his skin:

> "You shall also make a plate of pure gold and shall engrave on it, like the engravings of a seal, 'Holy to the LORD'.
> And you shall fasten it on a blue cord, and it shall be on the turban; it shall be at the front of the turban.
> And it shall be on Aaron's forehead… And it shall always be on his forehead" (Ex 28:36-38)

As you can see, this gold plate was to be marked "like the engravings of a seal". As already noted, in those days metal seals were pressed into wet clay or warm wax as a mark of ownership or to authenticate documents, pottery and valuable goods. The gold plate, worn on Aaron's forehead and engraved with His name, was therefore God's own signature, proclaiming that Aaron was His man, set apart to be the High Priest.

Obviously, once Aaron accepted this role, if he refused to wear the garments bearing the gold plate, he would no longer have the seal of God's ownership on him; if he became unholy like his two sons, Nadab and Abihu, he would suffer the consequences just as they did (Lev 10:1-3. See also Eli's sons in 1 Sam 2:30).

Isaiah's "Name on the Hand"

About eight hundred years later, we see again the wearer's free-will choice of God as owner – Isaiah predicts a time when a new generation of Israelites will choose to be named as Israel, the people of God:

> This one will say, "I am the LORD's",
> And that one will call on the name of Jacob;
> And another will write on his hand, "Belonging to the LORD",
> And will name Israel's name with honour. (Isa 44:5)

Like the plate on Aaron's forehead, this mark on the individual's hand is to signify to whom he *wants to belong*. It is clearly poetic or metaphorical rather than literal because, as we saw, the Law forbade tattooing. This also means the wearer can change his or her mind and turn back, as David warns us in Psalm 95:7-11, Jesus in Luke 9:62 and Paul in Romans 11:22. As for wanting to identify with or belong to Him, Paul is quite specific:

> 12. If we endure, we will also reign with Him;
> If we *deny Him*, He also will *deny us*;
> 13. If we are faithless, He remains faithful, for He cannot deny Himself (2 Tim 2:12-13, emphasis added)

It is not a matter of God changing His mind but of His allowing us to choose – if we repudiate His ownership, the mark is removed.

Of course, whenever God judged the nation of Israel as an unfaithful nation, there were always faithful individuals: 'the remnant', as Paul reminds us (Rom 9:27 and 11:5). They were protected, warned to flee or used to restore Israel. This also ensured that after an unfaithful generation had passed away, like those in the wilderness, the Lord could begin again with the next generation:

> 10. So the LORD's anger burned in that day, and He swore,
> saying,
> 11. "None of the men who came up from Egypt, from twenty
> years old and upward, shall see the land which I swore to
> Abraham, to Isaac and to Jacob; for they did not follow Me fully,
> 12. except Caleb the son of Jephunneh the Kenizzite and Joshua
> the son of Nun, for they have followed the LORD fully."
> 13. So the LORD's anger burned against Israel, and He made
> them wander in the wilderness forty years, until the entire
> generation of those who had done evil in the sight of the LORD
> was destroyed. (Num 32:10-13)

This meant that each individual could choose, like Caleb and Joshua, to be the Lord's, even if everyone else chose not to be.

Ezekiel's "Mark on the Forehead"

Just before the Babylonians breached the walls of Jerusalem in 586 B.C., Ezekiel heard of a mark of God being put on the foreheads of His people. He also heard why:

> And the LORD said to him [an angel], "Go through the midst of
> the city, even through the midst of Jerusalem, and put a mark
> [Heb. *tav*] on the foreheads of those who sigh and groan over all
> the abominations which are being committed in its midst".
> But to the others [six destroying angels] He said in my hearing,
> "Go through the city after him and strike; do not let your eye
> have pity, and do not spare.
> "Utterly slay old men, young men, maidens, little children, and
> women, but do not touch anyone on whom is the mark…"
> (Ezek 9:4-6, comments added)

We are not told what the mark looked like but the Hebrew word used is the Hebrew letter *tav*. Today it looks similar to the Greek letter *pi*, as you can see in fig. (ii), but in Ezekiel's time, it was represented as 'two sticks crossed to mark a place'.[39]

---

39 www.ancient-hebrew.org/3_taw.html, 29 May, 2013. My thanks to Elizabeth Rowe for this.

Figure (ii) Hebrew letter tav

We still use this concept today, in 'X marks the spot'. Not so commonly, we also can still use X as a signature,[40] which is how *tav* is actually translated in Job 31:35.

It is therefore very likely that the people were marked with a sign of a cross. Whether it was or not, Ezekiel would have understood it to be the Lord's signature or mark of ownership. Since it was only for the destroying angels to see, rather than the Israelites or Babylonians, we can assume it was invisible to everyone else.

Who received it? Everyone with a particular attitude, i.e. all who mourned the idolatry of their nation. This invisible mark would, however, have been visible to any who knew these people well; they could identify them as God's people from their attitudes and lifestyle.

John's "Seal on the Forehead"

This brings us up to John's day. In Revelation 7, John has a similar vision to Ezekiel's:

> 2. And I saw another angel ascending from the rising of the sun, having the seal of the living God; and he cried out with a loud voice to the four angels to whom it was granted to harm the earth and the sea,
> 3. saying, "Do not harm the earth or the sea or the trees until we have *sealed* the bond-servants of our God *on their foreheads*."
> 4. And I heard the number of those who were sealed, one hundred and forty-four thousand sealed from every tribe of the sons of Israel… (Rev 7:2-4, emphasis added)

Those marked are the same one hundred and forty-four

---

40 http://lawbrain.com/wiki/%22X%22_as_a_Signature, 29 May, 2013.

  Gotta Serve Somebody

thousand described in Revelation 14, so we will return to them in some detail later. For now, let us simply note that while the text does not specify whether this seal was visible or invisible, like those on Aaron and also on Ezekiel's remnant, it was 'the seal [Greek, *sphragis*] of the living God', i.e. the personal ownership signature or authentication of God Himself. As in Ezekiel's vision, it is to tell the angels whom they are to spare (vv. 2-3).

Then in Revelation 9, when the fifth trumpet sounds, John sees some bizarre locusts who can inflict 'the torment of a scorpion when it stings a man' (v. 5):

> 3. Then out of the smoke came locusts upon the earth, and power was given them, as the scorpions of the earth have power.
> 4. They were told not to hurt the grass of the earth, nor any green thing, nor any tree, but only the men who do not have the *seal of God on their foreheads*.
> (Rev 9:3-4, emphasis added)

Again we see the seal is to protect those marked, this time from the locust-scorpions.

John's "Name on the Forehead"

The last mention of an ownership mark is at the end of the Book of Revelation, in the last chapter of the New Testament. John sees 'the holy city, new Jerusalem' in 'a new heaven and a new earth' (Rev 21:1-2) in which…:

> 3. There will no longer be any curse; and the throne of God and of the Lamb will be in it, and His bond-servants will serve Him;
> 4. they will see His face, and His *name will be on their foreheads*.
> 5. …and they will reign forever and ever.
> (Rev 22:3-4, emphasis added)

Obviously, this vision is of a time still in the future for us all, at the time when all judgements are finished. Since the first curse was on Adam and Eve, bringing death and decay to the whole of Creation, the end of all curses will be after the Resurrection when, as John Donne proclaims, death itself will die.

This mark is on 'His bond-servants' who are *all the saints* in the new Creation where, at last, God's kingdom will have come and His will will continually be done.

This mark was also described at the beginning of Revelation where it is easily overlooked:

> 12. "He who overcomes, I will make him a pillar in the temple of My God, and he will not go out from it anymore; and I will *write* on him *the name of My God,* and *the name of the city* of My God, the new Jerusalem, which comes down out of heaven from My God, and *My new name.*" (Rev 3:12, emphasis added)

Not called a mark nor is its location described, its nature can be inferred from the chiasmic[41] structure of Revelation to be the same mark: in Revelation 3, the name of the Father, new Jerusalem and Jesus is written on everyone who overcomes; in Revelation 22, the name of God and of the Lamb is written on the inhabitants of New Jerusalem.

Given that the other reward for perseverance is to be made an immovable "pillar in the temple" (v. 12), i.e. metaphorical, it does seem these names are also written metaphorically rather than literally.

Summary of these Marks

Ownership marks were thoroughly familiar to both the ancient Jews and the 1st Century church, being described throughout the Old Testament:

---

41 'A chiasm is a repetition of similar ideas in the reverse sequence. The importance of the chiastic structure is found in its hidden emphasis' which is usually in the very centre, e.g. Isaiah 6:10, Matthew 6:24, 11:28-30. Thomas B. Clarke, www.bible-discernments.com/joshua/whatisachiasm.html, 6 Jun, 2013. Revelation being a chiasm means its principal focus is in chapter 12, the subject of Book 1, *Dancing in the Dragon's Jaws.*

(i)   The first mark of God was on Cain. While it is not described in any way, we know the infamous interpretation, that God cursed him with black skin to ensure that all his descendants were enslaved, is racist nonsense. This mark was actually to tell everyone who came across Cain that he was under God's protection.

(ii) In the 15th Century B.C., Aaron was called to wear the name of the Lord, "like the engravings of a seal" i.e. God's own signature, on his forehead. This authentication of Aaron as the holy high priest was voluntary and could be removed. If he had chosen to become unholy, as two of his sons had, he would have forfeited God's protection and been judged as they were.

(iii) In the 7th Century B.C., Isaiah spoke of Israelites writing the name of God on their hands to show they wanted to be identified as His people. This was clearly metaphorical as they were forbidden to tattoo themselves.

(iv) In the 6th Century B.C., Ezekiel saw an angel putting a mark or signature on the foreheads of all who were grieved at the idolatry of Israel. This angelic mark saved them from being killed when the Babylonians captured Jerusalem and seemed to have been visible only to God, the angels and possibly to Ezekiel as a prophet.

Ownership marks were also familiar in New Testament times, both from hand-written signatures and from signet rings pressed into wax or clay seals:

(i)   These literal marks were to authenticate documents and letters like Paul's.

(ii) In about 100 A.D., John saw 144,000 being sealed on the forehead by an angel with 'the seal of the living God', seemingly metaphorically or spiritually.

(iii) He also saw that all the saints who overcome will have the name of God and of the Lamb and of New Jerusalem written or 'sealed' on their foreheads metaphorically. This implies that the 144,000 have an additional calling.

Besides these, however, there were six more that were particularly important and *each of these still applies spiritually to all of us today.*

3

Six Marks, Four Texts
and Phylacteries

From the very beginning of God's creating the nation of Israel, He placed marks of His ownership on them, each mark revealing an essential issue of what it meant to be His people. In His extraordinary plan, as we will see, they also foreshadowed the essential issues of how we are to be true or genuine followers of Jesus today.

The first mark was literal, visible, historical and non-repeatable: the blood of the Passover lamb, placed on the threshold of Israelite homes in Egypt in the 15th Century B.C.

The second was the annual commemoration of that event, the Jewish festival of *Pesach* or Passover, which is still being kept to this day. This mark was not a literal mark but *metaphorical and invisible*, visible only as an activity or *behaviour*.

Conversely, anyone not participating was also 'marked' as *not* belonging to God:

> "But the man who… neglects to observe the Passover, that person shall then be cut off from his people, for he did not present the offering of the LORD at its appointed time. That man will bear his sin." (Num 9:13)

These two marks led to four more on every Israelite – all metaphorical and invisible, visible only as behaviours and outworked attitudes, and these four are described as being *on the foreheads and hands* of every individual willing to take part.

The first two of these, i.e. marks three and four, were also established at the time of the Exodus and were to be practised in perpetuity. Then forty years later, when Israel came to enter the Promised Land, God prescribed two more marks to be practised for all time.

These latter four 'marks', all written as *oth* in Hebrew, were considered by the Jews to be so important that, in a misguided bout of literalism during the intertestamental period,[42] some began to keep the four relevant texts of Scripture in phylacteries. Phylacteries, or tefillin as they call them today, are little leather boxes which Orthodox Jews tie on to their hands and foreheads.

Photo (i) Phylacteries or tefillin

As strange as this may seem today to those of us who are Gentiles, they were simply taking the four texts literally rather than metaphorically and trying to work around the prohibition against tattooing them on to their skin.

Happily, as we will see, there never was a need for phylacteries but they do provide an extraordinary illustration regarding the marks of God and of the beast.

The four texts are Exodus 13:1-10 and 13:11-16, and Deuteronomy 6:4-9 and 11:13-21. Their relevance to us today will also become crystal clear. Right now, however, we need to focus on the first mark, made with the blood of the Passover lamb.

---

42 The period between the last records of the Old Testament and the first events of the New, i.e. between about 420 and 5 B.C.

    Gotta Serve Somebody

The Passover's Mark on Houses

The mass exodus of the Jews from Egypt in 1446 B.C.[43] was not just a lucky escape or random act of kindness. God tells them why He acted:

> 4. "You yourselves have seen what I did to the Egyptians, and how I bore you on eagles' wings, and brought you to Myself.
> 5. "Now then, if you will indeed obey My voice and keep My covenant, then you shall be My own possession among all the peoples, for all the earth is Mine;
> 6. and you shall be to Me a kingdom of priests and a holy nation"
> (Ex 19:4-6)

They were to be God's own, unique, holy people,[44] to be a priestly nation among "all the peoples" (v. 5), i.e. Gentiles. His intention was that they would mediate between God in His holiness and everyone else in their unholiness. Accordingly, God placed His mark of authenticity and ownership on them. In verse 13 below, the Hebrew word, *oth*, is the same used for the mark on Cain:

> 12. "For I will go through the land of Egypt on that night, and will strike down all the firstborn in the land of Egypt, both man and beast; and against all the gods of Egypt I will execute judgments - I am the LORD.
> 13. "The blood shall be a sign [Heb, *oth*] for you on the houses where you live; and *when I see the blood I will pass over you,* and no plague will befall you to destroy you when I strike the land of Egypt…
>
> 23. "For the LORD will pass through to smite the Egyptians; and when He sees *the blood on the lintel and on the two doorposts,* the LORD will pass over the door and will not allow the destroyer to come in to your houses to smite you.
> (Ex 12:12-23, emphasis added)

---

43 The date of the Exodus is disputed, with some accepting 1446 B.C. (based on 1 Kings 6:1 and Solomon's ascension, thought to be in 961 B.C.) and others, about 1290 B.C. (based on their interpretation of some archaeological finds and absences).

44 See Revelation chapter 12 and Book 1, *Dancing in the Dragon's Jaws.*

The name Passover, Hebrew *Pesach*, comes from God 'passing over' every marked house so that the destroying angel could not enter it (v. 23). A similar description is given in Isaiah 31:5:

> Like flying birds so the LORD of hosts will protect Jerusalem.
> He will protect and deliver it; He will *pass over* and rescue it.

Just as in Ezekiel's vision, God used a mark to distinguish between those who were His and those who were not, but this particular ownership mark was literal and visible – it was made with blood. Carefully placed using a bunch of hyssop (Exo 12:22), it was daubed on the lintel and two doorposts of the threshold (v. 23).

And not just any blood – it was to be the blood of the Passover lamb or kid:

> 3. "Speak to all the congregation of Israel, saying, 'On the tenth of this month they are each one to take a lamb for themselves… a lamb for each household…
>
> 5. 'Your lamb shall be an unblemished male a year old; you may take it from the sheep or from the goats.
>
> 7. 'Moreover, they shall take some of the blood and put it on the two doorposts and on the lintel of the houses in which they eat it…
>
> 22. '… and none of you shall go outside the door of his house until morning'" (Ex 12:3-22)

The daubing of the lamb's blood on the thresholds by each household on the eve of the Exodus was a once-for-all time event and not to be repeated. At the annual commemorations, the Feast of Passover, the lambs were still to be ceremonially killed and eaten but the blood was instead poured out by the priests at the base of the altar of the Tabernacle and then of the Temple (Ezra 6:20).

The Passover's Mark on People

Equally as important as the blood on the house was the lamb's flesh being eaten by all inside the house:

> 8. "They shall eat the flesh that same night, roasted with fire, and they shall eat it with unleavened bread and bitter herbs.
> 9. 'Do not eat any of it raw or boiled at all with water, but rather roasted with fire, both its head and its legs along with its entrails.
> 10. 'And you shall not leave any of it over until morning, but whatever is left of it until morning, you shall burn with fire.'"
> (Ex 12:8-10)

This is not the place to properly consider this amazing prophetic drama but anyone interested can read more in *The Red Heifer's Ashes*.[45] Let us simply note that the lamb was to be completely consumed, either by the people or by the fire (v. 10), and the annual ritual was to be perpetual:

> 14. "Now this day will be a memorial to you, and you shall celebrate it as a feast to the LORD; throughout your generations you are to celebrate it as a permanent ordinance" (Ex 12:14)

On the first anniversary of the Exodus, as mentioned above, Moses included a stern warning:

> "But the man who… neglects to observe the Passover, that person shall then be cut off from his people, for he did not present the offering of the LORD at its appointed time. That man will bear his sin." (Num 9:13)

To "be cut off from his people" meant to be disowned, to no longer belong to the people of God.

Why was eating the lamb so important? Because it ensured that every individual had to choose every year to partake or not.

Keeping the annual Passover, therefore, was the second mark of God's ownership and it was on individuals. It was

---

45 Graeme Carlé, *The Red Heifer's Ashes (Mysteries of Ancient Israel)*, Emmaus Road Publishing, 2001.

voluntary, disappearing if anyone stopped keeping the Passover, but reappearing if they repented and started again. It was also a mark of the whole nation repenting and starting again, as seen during the reforms of Hezekiah (2 Chron 30:1ff) and Josiah (2 Kin 23:21-23) and when the returnees from Babylon renewed their commitment to Him (Ezra 6:19-22).

Relevance to Us Today

Three and a half thousand years later, this annual ritual is still being enacted by Orthodox Jews, showing they still want to be known as God's own people, to bear the second mark. Of course, in doing so, they demonstrate that they do not yet accept or understand that this astonishing Messianic prediction was perfectly fulfilled two thousand years ago by Jesus of Nazareth. John the Baptist was speaking to them, and us all, at Jesus' baptism:

> "Behold, the Lamb of God who takes away the sin of the world!" (John 1:29)

Likewise, Paul wrote to the Gentiles in Corinth:

> For Christ our Passover also has been sacrificed, let us therefore keep the feast… (1 Cor 5:7)

Peter too described believers as…:

> …redeemed… with precious blood, as of a lamb unblemished and spotless, the blood of Christ (1 Pet 1:18-19)

This revelation is the basis on which we overcome the enemy of our souls:

> And they [believers] overcame him [Satan] because of the blood of the Lamb and because of the word of their testimony… (Rev 12:11)

Every time our personal testimony is on our lips, *we are re-enacting Passover*, applying the blood to the threshold of our bodies, which are our earthly dwelling places, and thereby closing down Satan's right of entry. N.B. we are not re-offering the Passover but remembering what Jesus 'did once for all when He offered up Himself' (Heb 7:27).

Our trusting in Jesus' death on the cross is therefore the first mark of God's ownership on us today. This also means that those not yet trusting in Jesus have not yet received this mark, so we need to tell them.

The second mark is that we *keep on partaking* of the Lamb. Just as the Jews were to eat a lamb annually, we must keep eating spiritually:

> 53. So Jesus said to them, "Truly, truly, I say to you, unless you eat the flesh of the Son of Man and drink His blood, you have no life in yourselves.
> 54. "He who eats My flesh and drinks My blood has eternal life, and I will raise him up on the last day.
> 55. "For My flesh is true food, and My blood is true drink."
> (John 6:53-55)

Eating and drinking illustrates a profound spirituality because swallowing takes the morsel or liquid into the deepest parts of our being. This was never about a literal trans-substantiation[46] but a metaphor of how important it is that we 'receive Him' into every aspect of our life and being.

Accordingly, we celebrate His sacrifice of two thousand years ago when we partake of the Lord's Supper or communion

---

46 The belief that 'in the most blessed sacrament of the Eucharist the body and blood, together with the soul and divinity, of our Lord Jesus Christ and, therefore, the whole Christ is truly, really and substantially contained… It is a substantial presence by which Christ, God and man, makes himself wholly and entirely present… By the consecration of the bread and wine there takes place a change in the whole substance of the bread into the substance of the body of Christ our Lord and of the whole substance of the wine into the substance of his blood.' Article 1374, *Catechism of the Catholic Church*, 1994, English edition.

because He commands us: "Do this *in remembrance* of Me" (Luke 22:19). We thereby 'proclaim the Lord's death until He comes' (1 Cor 11:26). This is not now an annual event but as often as we want or feel the need to remind ourselves of what He did for us.

It is this *continuing* to receive the Lamb of God that is the second, metaphorical mark, demonstrating that we still belong to God.

Summary of the Two Marks of Passover

The first mark (Hebrew, *oth*) was given in Egypt three and a half thousand years ago and was:

(i)   Literal and visible. It was the blood of the Passover lamb.

(ii) Daubed "on the two doorposts and on the lintel of the houses" in which they ate it (Exo 12:7). It was to protect each household from losing their first-born males, "both man and beast" (v. 12), because the lamb took the place of their firstborn. The blood demonstrated that a vicarious death had already occurred in these homes.

(iii) A faith-based, free-will offering with clear consequences. Those trusting in Moses' prophecy needed to sacrifice the Passover lamb properly – if they had not placed the blood as commanded (v. 7) or if they had gone outside before the time (v. 22), there would have been no mark of God and therefore no protection.

(iv) The day itself was to become a permanent celebration to help them remember the event "throughout your generations" (v. 14). Again in v. 24: "observe this event as an ordinance for you and your children forever".

Exactly a year later, on the first anniversary of their liberation,

all of Israel accepted the second mark by keeping the annual
Feast of Passover:

(i)   This mark was not made literally with blood but was
      metaphorical. Moses warned that if anyone "neglects to
      observe the Passover, that person shall then be cut off
      from his people" (Num 9:13) so we see that continuing
      to observe the Passover was a mark of God's ownership.

(ii) It was a choice, requiring faith and faithfulness, to
      annually celebrate this unique event for all time.

(iii) Whereas the literal, visible Passover mark was only
      once on their houses and got them out of Egypt by
      households, the annual commemoration continued to
      mark every individual who chose to participate.

These two marks, literal and metaphorical, were signs of God's
ownership. They were followed by four more that God placed
on every individual Israelite and it is *the fourth we need to
understand in order to understand the mark of the beast.*

The Other Four Invisible Marks

These four are described as being on the hands and foreheads of
every Israelite who, after they observed the Passover, *continued
to live in four more particular ways.* These visible ways of life
were to set them apart as belonging to God as surely as if they
had the name of God written on their hand and forehead.
The four were:

(i)   The keeping of another annual festival with a special
      diet (Exo 13:1-10)

(ii) The sanctifying of the firstborn (Exo 13:11-16)

(iii) Loving and obeying God (Deut 6:4-9). This mark
includes the famous monotheistic creed of Israel, the
Shema: "Hear, O Israel! The LORD is our God, the LORD
is one!"

(iv) Avoiding deception (Deut 11:13-21).

4

Forehead & Hand
Eating & Honouring

The first mark on the forehead and hand of God's people required a week every year.

1. The Feast of Unleavened Bread

On the day after the Passover meal, every Israelite was to keep to a special diet:

> 6. For seven days you shall eat unleavened bread, and on the seventh day there shall be a feast to the LORD.
> 7. Unleavened bread shall be eaten throughout the seven days; and nothing leavened shall be seen among you, nor shall any leaven be seen among you in all your borders.
> 8. And you shall tell your son on that day, saying, "It is because of what the LORD did for me when I came out of Egypt".

Notice the effect:

> 9. And it shall serve as [lit. be] a sign [Heb. *oth*] to you on your hand, and as a reminder [Heb. *zikron*, a memorial] on your forehead, that the law of the LORD may be in your mouth; for with a powerful hand the LORD brought you out of Egypt.
> 10. Therefore, you shall keep this ordinance at its appointed time from year to year. (Ex 13:6-10)

The observance or keeping of this annual feast was to 'serve as', literally *be,* a sign or mark on their hands and foreheads of God's ownership. The Hebrew word, *oth,* is the same as was used in Genesis 4 of Cain's mark and in Exodus 12 of the Passover lamb's blood.

In other words, their obedience would show they belonged to God as surely as if they had His name written on their hands and foreheads.

The observance was to be 'a reminder' (v. 9), year after year, of the One who had delivered them and of how they had come into existence as a nation. It ensured they remained distinct as a people.

As for the festival, it consisted entirely of a particular diet (v. 6). They could eat any grain, fruit and vegetables they liked, as well as their usual *kosher* meat as described in Leviticus 11. However, for the week after they had eaten the Passover lamb, all of Israel was to carefully avoid eating anything with leaven (i.e. yeast).

In summary:

(i)   Their annual observance of this festival was to be 'a sign' or mark of ownership to onlookers that those partaking belonged to God.

(ii) It was to be 'a reminder' ('memorial', *NIV*) of the Exodus, of how they had come into existence as a nation, so that they would remain distinct.

(iii) They did not receive a literal mark on their hands or foreheads; what marked them was their response to the command to keep this diet.

(iv) If they stopped observing this feast, the 'sign' or mark would be gone. They would no longer be distinct and His mark of ownership would have disappeared.

What Does This Mean For Us Today?

This festival was a prophetic drama which Paul says was to foreshadow[47] a spiritual lifestyle for us:

> Clean out the old leaven, that you may be a new lump, just as you are in fact unleavened. For Christ our Passover also has been sacrificed.
> Let us therefore celebrate the feast, not with old leaven, nor with the leaven of malice and wickedness, but with the unleavened bread of sincerity and truth (1 Cor 5:7-8)

---

47   Colossians 2:16-17

                                                Gotta Serve Somebody

Just as all in Israel were to respond to the Passover lamb by getting rid of any leavened bread in their dwellings for a week, we today are to respond to Christ's sacrifice by getting rid of all 'malice and wickedness' in our hearts for as long as we live.

What exactly are these two attitudes? The Concise Oxford Dictionary defines malice as 'active ill will' or hatred while the original Greek word, *kakia,* is used in the New Testament mainly as 'a force that is destructive of fellowship'.[48] In other words, it is the lack of love. 'Wickedness' is a broader term meaning the deliberate doing of wrong; it is the opposite of righteousness.

So the mark of God on any of us today is that we are willing to deal with any malice and wickedness in our hearts i.e. *we are to be recognisable by our love and our righteous behaviour.* These two attitudes set us apart as God's people. And we are to 'celebrate the feast… with the unleavened bread of sincerity and truth', i.e. without pretence and in reality.

Lastly, and this is essential, we are not trying to live this way to earn our salvation. Israel's feast was a reminder that God had delivered them from Egypt because of the Passover lamb. In the same way, we are to deal with our leaven while remembering that Christ our Passover is the only sacrifice that can save us. As the saying goes, we are saved *to do* good works, not *by* good works.

John's Confirmation

Bob Dylan's song *Gotta Serve Somebody* spells out how every one of us is serving one of only two masters. He summarises: "It may be the devil or it may be the Lord, but you're gonna have to serve somebody!" There is simply no third option.

However, the apostle John spells out how we can recognise who it is we are really serving and who belongs to whom:

---

48 *Kittel's Theological Dictionary of the New Testament,* Abridged, p. 391.

In Biblical thinking, 'children of…' was a common metaphor indicating 'belonging to' or 'characterised by', e.g. children of wrath (Eph 2:3), children of light (Eph 5:8). In this instance, the ownership marks of both masters 'are obvious', being seen in how we outwork righteousness and love: anyone belonging to God will 'practise righteousness' and 'love his brother'; anyone belonging to the devil will not.

Regarding this love, Jesus had earlier taught:

By this all men will know that you are My disciples, if you have love for one another (John 13:35)

This is not love for our own family members but for all those in God's family, the household of faith – loving His disciples is often much harder.

Regarding righteousness, Paul specifically called it a mark or 'seal':

the firm foundation of God stands, having this seal… "Let everyone who names the name of the Lord abstain from wickedness" (2 Tim 2:19)

So, if we want to know to whom people belong, we are to consider: *are they trying to live righteously* and *do they love Jesus' disciples?* These two behaviours make it, in John's words, 'obvious', or in Jesus' and Paul's, they reveal and are a 'seal', or ownership mark, on those who are truly God's people.

Personally, I have found this a very practical help in understanding any of my friends, neighbours or workmates who are either in cults (they try to be righteous but are unloving towards outsiders) or living in compromise (they try to be loving but avoid Biblical righteousness).

It is, and always will be, our choice as to how we live and whom we serve but, according to John, if we are not 'the children of God', we are 'the children of the devil'. Very few of us have ever consciously signed up with Satan but, tragically, that is our default position until we turn to Jesus, as John tells us elsewhere:

> He [Jesus] came to His own [the Jewish people], and those who were His own did not receive Him.
> But as many as received Him, to them He gave the right to become children of God, even to those who believe in His name (John 1:11-12)

Summary of the First 'Forehead & Hand Mark'

(i) From Israel's beginning as God's nation, He marked (Hebrew, *oth*) them on their hands and foreheads, not by literal marks such as tattoos but by their behaviour in keeping the Feast of Unleavened Bread.

(ii) This consisted of a week-long diet of abstaining from anything leavened. It began the day after they had eaten the Passover lamb, in response to their deliverance.

(iii) Paul says this foreshadows a spiritual lifestyle for all believers – if we are truly trusting in Christ, we will abstain from the metaphorical 'leaven' of malice and wickedness. In other words, we will always be trying to be loving and righteous.

(iv) John confirms that the distinguishing features of those who truly belong to God will be love and righteousness; those who belong to the devil will allow the opposite in their hearts, malice and wickedness.

(v) These marks are therefore attitudes, behaviours and character traits.

(vi) Both of these marks can disappear or reappear through a change of heart i.e. through apostasy or repentance.

2. Sanctifying the Firstborn

The second mark on the forehead and hand is also found in
Exodus 13:

> 11. Now it shall come about when the LORD brings you to the
> land of the Canaanite, as He swore to you and to your fathers,
> and gives it to you,
> 12. that you shall devote to the LORD the first offspring of every
> womb, and the first offspring of every beast that you own; the
> males belong to the LORD.
> 13. But every first offspring of a donkey you shall redeem with a
> lamb, but if you do not redeem it, then you shall break its neck;
> and every firstborn of man among your sons you shall redeem.
> 14. And it shall be when your son asks you in time to come,
> saying, "What is this?" then you shall say to him, "With a powerful
> hand the LORD brought us out of Egypt, from the house of
> slavery.
> 15. "And it came about, when Pharaoh was stubborn about
> letting us go, that the LORD killed every firstborn in the land
> of Egypt, both the firstborn of man and the firstborn of beast.
> Therefore, I sacrifice to the LORD the males, the first offspring of
> every womb, but the firstborn of my sons I redeem".
> 16. So it shall serve as a sign [Heb. *oth*] on *your hand,* and as
> phylacteries [Heb. *totafot*] on *your forehead,* for with a powerful
> hand the LORD brought us out of Egypt
> (Ex 13:11-16 emphasis added)

Like the first mark, it too directly related to the Passover
mark. Since the Passover blood saved the life of the firstborn
of every household, this metaphorical mark was to be their
grateful response. When every Israelite family had their first
son, they were to 'redeem' him by offering a special sacrifice,
and as every cow, ewe and nanny goat had her first male
offspring, the family was to sacrifice it by giving it to the
priests (Num 18:13-20).

Before we establish what this mark means for us today,
however, we need to address the mistranslation of v. 16 because
on first reading, it does *seem* to require phylacteries.

Phylacteries

As noted earlier, Orthodox Jews today prefer to call them tefillin, which comes from the Hebrew word for prayer, to avoid any thought of superstition:

> The etymology of the term "phylactery" (from the Greek, to guard against evil, to protect) indicates the meaning, in the Hellenistic period, to have been "amulet" (an object worn as a protection against evil)[49]

The Hebrew word is *totafot,* and its meaning today seems uncertain. Translating Exodus 13:16, the *NASB* has 'phylacteries' while the *NIV* uses 'symbol' and the *NRSV,* 'emblem'. Others have 'frontlets'[50] which can describe an amulet or ornament worn on the forehead or, in military terminology, the metal face-guard of a soldier which came down between the eyes.

However, there is a way to remove any ambiguity.

The Septuagint, the Greek translation of the Hebrew Old Testament, was made between 300 and 200 B.C.[51] When these Jewish scholars came to *totafot* in Exodus 13:16, Deuteronomy 6:8 and 11:18, the three passages we are going to consider, they chose the Greek word *asaleutos* which means something immovable.[52] This is also used twice in the Greek New Testament: firstly, when the prow of a ship struck a reef,

---

49 www.JewishEncyclopedia.com, 8 June, 2009.

50 *KJV, ASV, ESV, RSV, NKJV,* margin of *NRSV.*

51 Septuagint (or, LXX) is the name given to the Greek translation of the Hebrew Scriptures. Begun in Alexandria, Egypt, during the reign of Ptolemy Philadelphus (285-246 B.C.), it was widely used among Hellenistic Jews, many of whom were beginning to lose their use of Hebrew due to their dispersion. According to an ancient document, the *Letter of Aristeas*, the translation was made by 70 to 72 Jewish scholars, hence the name 'Septuagint' which means seventy in Latin. Jesus and the New Testament writers trusted it, quoting it for the majority of their Old Testament references, as did their audience, most of whom spoke and read Greek. www.septuagint.net/, 8 Jun, 2009.

52 www.jewishencyclopedia.com/view.jsp?artid=290&letter=P&search=phylactery#1109, 5 Jun, 2009.

'stuck fast and remained *immovable*' (Acts 27:41); secondly, to describe 'a kingdom which *cannot be shaken*' (Heb 12:28).

Accordingly, the Septuagint reading of Exodus 13:16 reads:

> So it [the sacrificing/redeeming of the firstborn] shall serve as [lit. be] a sign on your hand, and as *something immovable* on your forehead, for with a powerful hand the LORD brought us out of Egypt.

Compare this now with the parallel phrase in Exodus 13:9 in the Masoretic Text[53] which is unambiguous – the Feast was to be 'a reminder':

> And it [the Feast of Unleavened Bread] shall serve as [lit. be] a sign to you on your hand, and as *a reminder* [Heb. *zikkaron*] on your forehead, that the law of the LORD may be in your mouth; for with a powerful hand the LORD brought you out of Egypt [emphasis & comments added]

This would mean 'a reminder' is to be 'something immovable'. This is perfectly consistent with both rituals reminding all succeeding generations of two particular aspects of the Passover:

> Now this day will be a memorial to you, and you shall celebrate it as a feast to the LORD; throughout your generations you are to celebrate it as a permanent ordinance (Ex 12:14)

We can therefore safely conclude that all three of these ordinances are to be 'a memorial' or 'reminder' that is 'permanent', 'throughout your generations' and 'immovable'.

Notice the effect of Exodus 13:16 – the keeping of the command was 'to serve as [lit. *be*] a sign' and 'as something immovable'. In other words, instead of wearing a physical object as an amulet or for protection, they only needed to

---

53 The authoritative Hebrew text, named after the Masoretes, i.e. the mostly Karaite scholars and scribes who between the 7th and 11th Centuries preserved the ancient texts and devised a vowel notation system for the Hebrew language.

                                          Gotta Serve Somebody

keep offering the firstborn to God and they would be marked.

We will return to phylacteries soon. Let us just note for now that this second mark was to be a continual reminder of how God had spared Israel's firstborn. This was *not on the basis of their wearing leather boxes, but by their offering the Passover lamb as if it were the firstborn.*

Summary of the Second 'Forehead & Hand Mark'

Exodus 13:16 can be summarised as follows:

(i)   Israel's continuing to sanctify the first-born male was a sign or mark of God's ownership on their hands.

(ii)   It would also be as a memorial on their foreheads to remind them of their deliverance because of the Passover lamb sacrifice.

(iii)   They did not receive a literal mark on their hands or foreheads.

(iv)   What marked them as belonging to God was their voluntary response to His ordinance.

(v)   If they stopped acknowledging the firstborn, the 'sign' and the 'reminder' would be gone so this mark of God's ownership would be removed from them.

Relevance for Us Today

This second mark was as overtly messianic as the Passover lamb – everyone redeeming their first-born son with that lamb was prefiguring and looking forward to the coming of Messiah, Jesus, as the Firstborn of God.

Paul explains:

> He is the image of the invisible God, the firstborn of all creation... and the firstborn from the dead; so that He Himself might come to have first place in everything
> (Col 1:15 & 18)

Notice that although Jesus is explicitly God made visible, He is also 'the firstborn of all creation'.

To the Jews, the first-born son had particular privileges and responsibilities. For example, when the father died, he was to receive a double portion of the family's inheritance (Deut 21:17) and to look after the mother. This means that Jesus is the principal Heir to receive all of creation.[54] He is also the firstborn of the resurrection and 'to have first place in everything', which means to be worshipped as God. The Father has always intended..:

> "… that all will honour the Son, even as they honour the Father. He who does not honour the Son does not honour the Father who sent Him" (John 5:22-23)

It is this honouring of the Son 'even as', or in the exact same way as, we honour the Father that marks us as belonging to Him, hence the vast importance of the doctrine of the Trinity. Paul explains further:

> No one can say, "Jesus is Lord", except by the Spirit of God (1 Cor 12:3)

In other words, we need supernatural revelation to truly see who He is. This revelation, also identified by Jesus in Matthew 16:13-20, marks each of us as truly belonging to God or not. It therefore marks as *not yet Christian* all individuals, movements or denominations who think they are Christian but deny the uniqueness of Jesus as God incarnate (e.g. Mormons, Jehovah's Witnesses, Christadelphians etc).

Lastly, this honouring or sanctifying is and always will remain a freewill decision for each of us, to live according to this revelation. Peter confirms it:

---

54 Some, like the Unitarians, Jehovah's Witnesses and Christadelphians, have thought 'firstborn' means Jesus was simply the first being to be created and therefore is not God. However, firstborn here refers to His primacy as the Heir. *Kittel's Theological Dictionary, Abridged*, 1990, p. 967-968.

Gotta Serve Somebody

What then of those who refuse to do that, who reject Jesus as God's Firstborn? Instead of acknowledging, honouring and 'sanctifying the firstborn', those who ignore His identity and message do not belong to God.

Some, meaning well, teach that we are all the children of God. For example, the extraordinary Mohandas Gandhi wrote of a discussion he had with Christians:

> It was more than I could believe that Jesus was the only incarnate son of God, and that only he who believed in him would have everlasting life. If God could have sons, all of us were His sons. If Jesus was like God, or God Himself, then all men were like God and could be God Himself.[55]

This autobiography was published in 1927, twenty-one years before he died, so he may have subsequently changed his mind. Personally, I fervently hope so, because I admire much of his character and life. However, whenever given a choice of who to believe, I will always choose Jesus, who had to explain the exact issue to the religious leaders of His day:

> 23. … "You are from below, I am from above; you are of this world, I am not of this world.
> 24. "Therefore I said to you that you will die in your sins; for unless you believe that I am He, you will die in your sins."
> 25. So they were saying to Him, "Who are You?" Jesus said to them, "What have I been saying to you from the beginning?"
> (John 8:23-25)

His identity is not a matter of personal preference but an essential for us to gain eternal life. He went on to explain what was going wrong in them:

> 41. …They said to Him, "We were not born of fornication; we have one Father: God."

---

55   M.K. Gandhi, *An Autobiography (The Story of My Experiments With Truth)*, London; Penguin Books, 1927, p. 135.

In response, many trusted in Him but others 'picked up stones to throw at Him' (John 8:59) before He escaped.

We have to understand just two more marks that God placed on the foreheads and hands of His people and then we will be able unpack the mark of the beast.

5

The Last Two
Loving & Avoiding

The third mark on the forehead and hand of God's people was an attitude.

3. Loving and Obeying God

Turning now to Deuteronomy 6, we come to the most famous words of Judaism, their essential doctrine or creed, the Shema, and the greatest commandment:

> 4. Hear, O Israel! The Lord is our God, the Lord is one!
> 5. And you shall love the LORD your God with all your heart and with all your soul and with all your might (Deut 6:4-5)

This foundational statement of monotheism is then followed by… a mark on the hand and on the forehead:

> 6. And these words, which I am commanding you today, shall be on your heart;
> 7. And you shall teach them diligently to your sons and shall talk of them when you sit in your house and when you walk by the way and when you lie down and when you rise up.
> 8. And you shall bind them as a sign [Heb. *oth*] on your hand and they shall be as frontals [Heb. *totafot*] on your foreheads.

Notice in v. 8, for the first time, binding or tying something on your hand *could* be taken literally, as could the following verse:

> 9. And you shall write them on the doorposts of your house and on your gates.

Just as they strap the tefillin or phylacteries to their bodies, Orthodox Jews and many non-Orthodox to this day still attach to their door-posts mezuzahs, little leather boxes holding just the twenty-two lines of this text.[56]

The question is, however, which 'words' did God want them to 'bind' on their hands and 'write' on their door-posts? All who try to literally fulfill these commandments sadly fall way short of literal obedience because 'these words, which I am commanding you today' were many more than the twenty-two lines in a mezuzah. Moses was again giving them the whole Law that day!

The binding and writing that God intended them to do was not literal, any more than it was in Proverbs:

> 20. My son, observe the commandment of your father
> And do not forsake the teaching of your mother;
> 21. Bind them continually on your heart;
> Tie them around your neck.
> 22. When you walk about, they will guide you;
> When you sleep, they will watch over you;
> And when you awake, they will talk to you.
> (Prov 6:20-22)

Are sons really to keep binding and tying on the outside of their bodies everything said to them by their fathers and mothers? Will these pieces of paper or leather really keep watch at night?

How about sticking them in their eyes?

> Keep my commandments and live,
> And my teaching as the apple [i.e. pupil] of your eye.
> Bind them on your fingers;
> Write them on the tablet of your heart
> (Prov 7:2-3)

No-one was ever expected to literally cover their pupils, tie words onto their fingers or tattoo their hearts. Instead, they (and we) are to live by the wisdom of mothers and fathers *by valuing and remembering* what they say.

In the same way, the ancient Israelites were not to, could

---

56 www.jewfaq.org/signs.htm, 13 Jun, 2011.

  Gotta Serve Somebody

not, bind the observance of festivals on to their bodies nor
to attach all the scrolls of the Law of Moses to their entrance
ways. Instead, they were to live according to the Law in
everything they did.

We can therefore summarise Deuteronomy 6:4-8 as follows:

(i)   Israel's daily loving of God and living according to all
      the words of Moses would be like tying or binding
      God's ownership mark (Hebrew, *oth)* on their hands.

(ii) These words were to affect them in everything they
      did.

(iii) They did not receive a literal mark on their hands or
      foreheads.

(iv) This lifestyle was an on-going voluntary response to
      His words.

(v)   If they stopped loving and obeying God, this mark of
      God's ownership would be removed from them.

Relevance for Us Today

This third invisible mark is also known as the greatest
commandment:

> One of them, a lawyer, asked Him [Jesus] a question, testing
> Him, "Teacher, which is the great commandment in the Law?"
> And He said to him, "'YOU SHALL LOVE THE LORD YOUR GOD WITH
> ALL YOUR HEART, AND WITH ALL YOUR SOUL, AND WITH ALL YOUR
> MIND'. This is the great and foremost commandment"
> (Matt 22:35-38, capitals in original to show Old Testament quote)

This whole-hearted love of God is acknowledged by the Jews
as their distinguishing mark but it should be also for every
professing follower of Jesus. He went on to add:

> "The second is like it, 'YOU SHALL LOVE YOUR NEIGHBOR AS
> YOURSELF'.
> On these two commandments depend the whole Law and the
> Prophets" (Matt 22:39-40)

Which brings us back to the primary application of Book 2, *Slouching Towards Bethlehem,* and Jesus telling us how we should respond:

> "But I say to you, love your enemies and pray for those who persecute you, so that you may be sons of your Father who is in heaven; for He causes His sun to rise on the evil and the good, and sends rain on the righteous and the unrighteous"
> (Matt 5:44-45)

What then of those not marked by the love of the Lord our God to do all that He wants us to do?

We must never forget the warning Jesus gave us in His famous sermon on the mount:

> 21. "Not everyone who says to Me, 'Lord, Lord,' will enter the kingdom of heaven, but he who does the will of My Father who is in heaven will enter.
> 22. "Many will say to Me on that day, 'Lord, Lord, did we not prophesy in Your name, and in Your name cast out demons, and in Your name perform many miracles?'
> 23 "And then I will declare to them, 'I never knew you; DEPART FROM ME, YOU WHO PRACTICE LAWLESSNESS.' (Matt 7:21-23)

In v. 23, where Jesus is quoting Psalm 6:8, He rebukes 'lawlessness' or iniquity. This is the hallmark of 'the man of lawlessness' or iniquity (2 Thess 2:3), as we saw in *Slouching Towards Bethlehem* regarding the Antichrist. The contrast is stark and absolute: either we are doing the will of our Father who is in heaven or we are lawless; either we belong to God or we are like 'the man of lawlessness'.

Notice, too, we can change marks any time:

> 6. Let no one deceive you with empty words, for because of these things the wrath of God comes upon the sons of disobedience.
> 7. Therefore do not be partakers with them;
> 8. for you were formerly darkness, but now you are light in the Lord; walk as children of light
> 9. (for the fruit of the light consists in all goodness and

righteousness and truth),
10. trying to learn what is pleasing to the Lord.
(Eph 5:6-10)

We all used to be sons or children of disobedience but now as believers, we are to bear this mark of belonging to God. If, however, we choose to again become lawless and disobedient to God, we will lose His mark.

4. Avoiding Deception

The fourth mark is the one we need to understand to understand the mark of the beast.

It is described in Deuteronomy 11:

16. Beware, lest your hearts be deceived and you turn away and serve other gods and worship them.
17. Or the anger of the LORD will be kindled against you, and He will shut the heavens so that there will be no rain and the ground will not yield its fruit; and you will perish quickly from the good land which the LORD is giving you.
18. You shall therefore impress these words of mine on your heart and on your soul; and you shall bind them as a sign [Heb. *oth*] on your hand, and they shall be as frontals [Heb. *totafot*, Lit. something immovable] on your foreheads.
19. And you shall teach them to your sons… (Deut 11)

We see in v. 18 that it is 'these words' that are to be the sign or mark and again the Hebrew, *oth,* is the same word as used in Cain's mark.

Now, consider the context.

Earlier, in Deuteronomy 11:2-7, Moses had reminded Israel of everything God had done for them and in vv. 8-12, what He was about to give them, the 'land of milk and honey'. He therefore urges them to love and serve God wholeheartedly (vv. 13-15) *but adds* that this includes remaining faithful to Him:

16. Beware, lest… you turn away and serve other gods and worship them (Deut 11:16)

Their faithfulness was to be seen in how they related to 'these words' of Moses (v. 18), Moses being the prophet and mediator of this covenant with God (Galatians 3:19). They were therefore to commit themselves heart and soul to what they were hearing:

> 18. You shall therefore impress these words of mine on your heart and on your soul; and you shall bind them as a sign on your hand, and they shall be as *totafot* [Heb. something immovable] on your foreheads. (Deut 11:18)

The first part of this command, to 'impress these words… on your heart and on your soul', is clearly metaphorical. The second part, to 'bind them on your hand', could be metaphorical or literal and the phylactery-wearers took it literally.

However, as we saw in establishing the proper meaning of *totafot* as a memorial or reminder, this ambiguity can be resolved – their behaviour in obeying 'these words' *is* the mark on their hands and foreheads.

Moses goes on in Deuteronomy 12 to warn them of the idolatry of the land they were about to enter: the shrines (v. 2); the idols (v. 3); and the cultic sacrifices (v. 13), which included the Canaanites killing their own children (v. 31). Summarising with "Beware that you are not ensnared to follow them" (v. 30), he then reveals how the temptation would come – *from the arising of false prophets* (Deut 13).

It is here that we, at last, come to see *the relevance of the mark of the beast.*

This fourth invisible mark is seen in how Israel identifies and shuns the idolatry offered by the false prophets.

Responding to the False Prophet

We have now come full circle, back to Deuteronomy 13 which we considered in Book 2, *Slouching Towards Bethlehem*. This text called on everyone in ancient Israel to beware of false prophets with signs and wonders and therefore, ultimately, the spirit of antichrist:

> 1. If a prophet or a dreamer of dreams arises among you and gives you a sign or a wonder
> 2. and the sign or the wonder comes true, concerning which he spoke to you, saying, "Let us go after other gods (whom you have not known) and let us serve them",
> 3. you shall not listen to the words of that prophet or that dreamer of dreams; for the LORD your God is testing you to find out if you love the LORD your God with all your heart and with all your soul.
> 4. You shall follow the LORD your God and fear Him; and you shall keep His commandments, listen to His voice, serve Him, and cling to Him. (Deut 13:1-4)

We saw in that study:

> This was the ultimate test of Israel's love for God. A sham miracle they could easily reject but a true wonder attributed to another god? Would they continue to choose the God of Abraham, Isaac and Jacob, to love Him with all their heart and soul? Would they look past the appearance even of supernatural signs and wonders to discern what was actually being said and proposed for worship? [57]

We also considered then:

> Why did He set this test? Because even with the newest married couple who have just begun to know each other intimately, both husband and wife can validly expect the other to not wander off with someone else. Look again at what the false prophet would be saying to lead Israel astray: "Let us go after other gods (whom you have not known) and let us serve them" (Deut 13:2)

---

57 *Slouching Towards Bethlehem*, p. 79.

Moses' inserted comment, 'whom you have not known', was the key to their passing this test. Having come to know God, they were not to wander off to serve another. Just as survivors of a sinking ship will not let go the floating wreckage, all in Israel were to 'cling to Him' (v. 4).[58]

There is, therefore, an exact and deliberate parallel between Moses' generic warning about 'a prophet' and John's visions of 'the false prophet' (Rev 16:13, 19:20 and 20:10). John's is specifically the spirit of antichrist manifesting in the Caesars of his day and in many emperors since, as we have identified in a number of despotic political leaders in the 20th Century. It will ultimately manifest in *the* Antichrist.

Summary of the Fourth 'Forehead & Hand Mark'

(i)   Israel's avoiding of idolatry and holding fast to the covenant would be tying 'a sign [Hebrew, *oth*] on [their] hand'.

(ii) This would also be as *'totafot* [i.e. an immovable memorial or reminder] on [their] forehead'.

(iii) Israel did not receive a literal mark on their hands or foreheads. What actually marked them as belonging to God was their voluntary response to His words regarding idolatry.

(iv) If they turned away to serve and worship other gods, the sign and the reminder would be gone and this fourth mark of God's ownership would thereby be removed from them.

(v)   In particular, Israel were to avoid being deceived by false prophets who came with supernatural signs and wonders.

---

58   Ibid.

(vi) Given the appearance of so many antichrists in the political arena in the last one hundred years and with the last one yet to come, this mark of God is particularly important today – its counterpart is the mark of the beast.

6

Inside the Box
Misguided Zeal

We now come to consider more closely that intriguing phenomenon in Jewish thinking – the invention and wearing of phylacteries. These little leather boxes were to be strapped on to the foreheads and arms of the faithful and, as we will see, they provide us with a wonderful illustration of the present confusion regarding the mark of the beast.

Photo (ii) Wearing phylacteries or tefillin
(courtesy of Rory Cavanagh)

Gotta Serve Somebody

As noted earlier, Orthodox Jews today prefer to call them *tefillin* because phylactery has an associated sense of superstition as in an amulet. Tefillin comes from the Hebrew for prayer (although one noted authority, Rabbi Louis Jacobs, insists its root word was to attach, or to distinguish, i.e. from Gentiles).[59]

While the total number of commandments in the written Law is held to be 613 to live by, in the oral tradition there are *hundreds* more regarding tefillin alone, i.e. their size, colour, manner of manufacture including the correct leather, thread and stitching, placement, times of wearing, even wear and tear, while the internal scrolls have to be perfectly inscribed using particular ink on particular parchment.[60]

Some today claim that Jesus would have worn phylacteries, that His reproof of the scribes and Pharisees for "broadening their phylacteries… to be noticed by men" (Matt 23:5) was only to address their ostentation. Not so. Jesus also asked them why they were accepting oral traditions instead of the Scriptures, and warned them:

> "Why do you yourselves transgress the commandment of God for the sake of your tradition?… You invalidated [or, made of no effect] the word of God for the sake of your tradition"
> (Matt 15:3-6)

Phylacteries or tefillin were not invented until after the Babylonian exile, when some overly-zealous Jews set aside the existing metaphorical understanding of the four texts described above and began to take them literally. It is not clear when exactly this was:

> The earliest explicit reference to phylacteries in a literary work is the Letter of Aristeas, section 159, where only the phylactery of the hand is mentioned. Scholars differ as to the dating of this text. Most place it in the 2nd century

---

59 *Concise Companion to the Jewish Religion*, Oxford University Press, 1999.
60 See, for example, www.beingjewish.com/mitzvos/tefillin.html, 30 Jun, 2013.

BCE, though some claim that parts of it, including sections
128-71, date from the 1st century CE.[61]

The *Jewish Encyclopedia* says they were invented earlier, in 'the
time of the Soferim [i.e. scribes] – the 4th, or at least the 3rd
Century B.C.'[62]

What is clear, however, is that a group of Pharisees set
aside a thousand years of historical practice which accepted
these texts as metaphors. Instead, they wrote out the four texts
and placed one each in the four compartments of the leather
boxes. To resolve the problem of trying to bind these words
of God on to their foreheads, hands and hearts, they placed
the one for the hand on the upper left arm so that it was over
the heart as well.

Why did they do it? The *Jewish Encyclopedia* explains it was
because of oral traditions:

> There are more laws – ascribed to oral delivery by God to
> Moses – clustering about the institution of tefillin than
> about any other institution of Judaism (… Maimonides
> mentions ten; Rodkinssohn mentions eighteen…). Thus,
> even if most Jewish commentators are followed in their
> literal interpretations of the Biblical passages mentioned
> above, rabbinic interpretation and traditional usage must
> still be relied upon for the determination of the nature of
> the tefillin and the laws concerning them.[63]

In other words, they explain away the Scriptures not
mentioning tefillin on the grounds that Moses is supposed to
have also given them a separate oral law which only the rabbis

---

61   Hakham Rekhavi, *A Sign Upon Your Hand and as Frontlets Between Your Eyes*, www.karaite-corner.org, 29 May, 2009.
Note: BCE (Before Common Era) and CE (Common Era) avoids using B.C. Before Christ and A.D. *Anno Domine* (*lit.* 'Year of our Lord').
62   www.jewishencyclopedia.com/view.jsp?artid=290&letter=P&search=phylactery#1109, Epoch of Introduction, 5 Jun, 2009.
63   www.jewishencyclopedia.com/view.jsp?artid=290&letter=P&search=phylactery#1109, Legal View, 5 Jun, 2009.

Gotta Serve Somebody

know and which adds in what the Scriptures are supposedly missing (including Moses giving them a separate oral law!). How similar this is to the Roman Catholic teaching that only their church traditions could explain the Scriptures.[64] In both cases, this means the people are not to accept any Scriptures that contradict the oral traditions – as Jesus said, their traditions nullify the written word of God (Matt 15:3-9).

Hakham Rekhavi is a Karaite Jew (Heb. *karaim,* Scripturalists or followers of Scriptures), believing in the Old Testament Scriptures alone and rejecting the Jewish oral traditions. The Karaites' rule of Biblical interpretation is that 'we must work hard to understand the "plain meaning" of the words understood naturally by the ancient Israelites'. Rekhavi explains further:

> … the wearing of phylacteries was seen as one of the criteria distinguishing a haver (member of the rabbinic "society") from an 'am haares (one not observing rabbinic customs). According to Josephus, himself a Pharisee, there were only about 6,000 of them in Israel during the late Second Temple period (Ant. 7:2:4), out of a possible Jewish population in Israel of some 2,000,000. Thus the 'am haares formed the overwhelming majority of the population, and the wearing of phylacteries was limited to a small group.[65]

In other words, phylacteries were a distinguishing mark on those 'observing the rabbinic customs' or traditions, which Jesus explicitly rejected (Mark 7:1-8).

The Karaites also reject phylacteries:

> The Torah commands us to treasure the commandments as jewels, not to strap leather amulets on to our heads and arms.[66]

---

64 'Both Scripture and Tradition must be accepted and honored with equal sentiments of devotion and reverence.' *Catechism of the Catholic Church,* para 82.
65 www.karaites.org.uk/phylacteries.shtml, 29 May, 2009.
66 www.karaite-korner.org/karaite-faq.shtml, 29 May, 2009.

We see then that the *haver* Jews began misinterpreting these metaphorical marks of God as literal because they came to rely on their oral traditions instead of on the Scriptures. Ironically, many in the church today are making the same mistake regarding the mark of the beast, and for the same reason.

The Forehead and the Hand

Why were these marks or signs described as being on the forehead and the hand? Besides the forehead being highly visible, both locations had a particular significance to the ancient Israelites. The head typified autonomy ('headship') or leadership,[67] as can be seen in Deuteronomy 28:13:

> The LORD shall make you the head and not the tail, and you only shall be above, and you shall not be underneath, if you will listen to the commandments….

This head/tail metaphor is taken from Israel's herd animals which, being four-footed, always had their heads leading the way for the tail to follow. The promise of God to Israel was that if they would obey Him, they would stay free from slavery to men, be leaders instead of followers, 'above' rather than 'underneath'. Accordingly, a mark on their foreheads signified their free-will or autonomy, that their obedience to God was always voluntary.

The hand typified their works:

> Whatever your hand finds to do, verily, do it with all your might (Eccl 9:10)

---

67 This concept is covered in some depth in the author's *Because of the Angels*, 1998.

    Gotta Serve Somebody

The right hand was particularly significant as a metaphor. Since most people are right-handed, their right hand is usually stronger, e.g. 'by His right hand and by His strong arm' (Isa 62:8), and more skilful than their left, e.g. 'If I forget you, O Jerusalem, may my right hand forget her skill' (Psa 137:5).

This led to the common concept of the favourite being 'seated at the right hand' (Psa 110:1, Matt 26:64). Remember Joseph trying to correct his father, Jacob, who had crossed his hands to ensure his right hand went on the head of Ephraim instead of Manasseh, the firstborn (Gen 48:8-20).

The right hand was also the one extended towards others (2 Sam 20:9, Psa 26:10, Gal 2:9) so the metaphorical mark of God's ownership was implicitly considered to be on their right hand rather than on their left.

Ironically, while Orthodox Jews today bind the head tefillin on their foreheads, they usually bind the hand tefillin above the elbow inside their *left* arm, unless the wearer is left-handed in which case it goes on the right.[68] They explain this as 'binding our minds with our hearts and deeds'.[69]

As sincere as this symbolism may be, it further illustrates how tradition has drifted away from the Scriptures. If tefillin were necessary, they should actually be on the outside of the right hand to maximise the visibility.

To summarise then, for Israel to be marked on their foreheads and hands signified that all their choices and actions were to proclaim the will and works of God as their Master and Owner. This prefigured Paul's exhortation to Christians:

> Whatever you do in word or deed, do all in the name of the Lord Jesus (Col 3:17)

---

68 www.beingjewish.com/mitzvos/tefillin.html, 1 Jul, 2013. See photo (ii)
69 www.chabad.org/generic_cdo/aid/102436/jewish/Tefillin.htm, 8 Jun, 2009.

Summary of the Marks of God, Before 30 A.D.[70]

To understand the mark of the beast as revealed to John in about 100 A.D., we first need to understand that it is the demonic counterpart of one of the marks of God. These marks were recorded throughout the Old Testament, the Early Church's primary written source, so they would have been readily understood by John's original hearers since their first leaders were all Jewish disciples or had been taught by them.

Today, we need to catch up, to become familiar with that overview as revealed over the millennia of Jewish history:

(i) The first ever mark was on Cain. Although there is no description of it, we do know it was to protect him from human vengeance. It may have been literal but seems more likely to have been a reputation or possibly a tangible sense of God's presence and protection.

(ii) In about 2000 B.C., God gave Abraham circumcision as a sign, mark or seal of the Abrahamic covenant. This was only ever on the males and foreshadowed the New Covenant's requirement to put off our flesh or carnal nature.

(iii) In 1446 B.C., God used Moses to make a covenant with the whole nation of Israel which included the weekly Sabbath, to be kept or observed within this covenant as a sign of His ownership. This foreshadowed the work of Christ Himself replacing our works.

(iv) Also in 1446 B.C., the gold plate on Aaron's forehead bore the name of the LORD. This engraving signified he had been set apart as High Priest and was put on with his garments. Aaron retained his free-will and could fulfill, reject or corrupt this calling, as had two of his sons.

---

70 The date of the Crucifixion. See *Dancing in the Dragon's Jaws*, p. 95.

(v)   Around 700 B.C., Isaiah wrote of Israelites metaphorically writing the LORD's name on their hand to signify their belonging to Him. We know this was not literal because they were forbidden tattoos; it was also voluntary and therefore removable.

(vi)   Just before 586 B.C., Ezekiel was told about angels marking all those in Jerusalem who would be protected when the Babylonian army broke in. This mark seems to have been visible only in the spiritual realm; the criterion for those marked was their faithfulness to God. It was therefore voluntary on their part and could be removed or restored.

We also saw a particular series of six marks:

(i)   At the Exodus, in 1446 B.C., God created a special mark, literal and visible to all, to protect all of Israel's first-born sons. This once-off mark was in blood, the blood of the Passover lamb, placed around the threshold of the homes of all trusting in Him (Exo 12).

(ii)   This literal mark in blood led to five more, but all metaphorical. The first of these metaphorical marks was the perpetual annual reminder in the Feast of Passover of that lamb's vicarious death. Every member of every household was to eat a portion of the lamb and if they chose to partake, they marked themselves as belonging to God; if they chose to not partake, they no longer had the mark (Num 9:13).

(iii) God then called them to receive two more marks which He said would be on their foreheads and hands (Exo 13). These were invisible and metaphorical marks: *to annually keep the Feast of Unleavened Bread* and *to continually sacrifice/redeem all first-born males*. Those keeping these two commands were thereby publicly seen to belong to God but those not keeping them, as not belonging to Him. These marks were obviously voluntary and could be removed or reaccepted, allowing anyone to walk away or to repent.

(iv) Forty years later, when Israel finally came to the Promised Land, God gave them two more commands to the same effect (Deut 6 and 11). One included Israel's primary creed, the Shema, urging Israel to mark themselves on their foreheads and hands *by lovingly obeying* the only true God; the other command was *to shun idolatry*, especially as promoted by false prophets with deceiving signs and wonders. Obviously, these too were voluntary.

(v) These latter four commands were of great significance to 1st Century Jews, and therefore John's original audience in the early church, as demonstrated in the invention of phylacteries two or three centuries before Christ. These little leather boxes contained the four texts and were strapped to the foreheads and arms of those misinterpreting the commands as literal rather than as metaphorical.

(vi) Ironically, in creating phylacteries, the haver Pharisees lost the four texts' essential connection with the Passover lamb and the Feast of Passover.

(vii) All six marks were to serve as highly visible marks of the invisible God's ownership. All were to express gratitude to Him who had delivered them out of Egypt. The metaphorical marks were described as being on the forehead and right hand to symbolise that His will was now to be expressed through everything they thought, said and did for their Owner and Master.

The Marks of God, After 30 A.D.

It took quite a while for the Early Church, though not Paul, to realise that their Old Covenant marks of God all foreshadowed the New Covenant's spiritual equivalents. For example, it was almost eighteen years before they all finally agreed at the great council in Jerusalem (circa 48 A.D.) that circumcision was no longer necessary for all male believers (Acts 15:1-29). They finally came to understand what God had been aiming for all along, that male circumcision foreshadowed both men and women putting aside sinful desires, just as Paul had been teaching (Col 2:11-13, Rom 2:25-29, Phil 3:3).

They *had* quickly grasped that just as God gave Israel the Passover lamb in 1446 B.C., He had in 30 A.D. given them Jesus as the real Passover lamb. It just took them time to understand what that meant for their new Gentile brothers and sisters.

Today, we who are Gentiles need to catch up with even their starting point, with what they would have understood about the six marks that, up until 30 A.D., showed who belonged to Him. Hopefully, in this book, we have now caught up.

We have also established the spiritual equivalent of all six marks, available to every one of us, whether Jew or Gentile. Since each is a voluntary behaviour, it is us, you and I, who are responsible for each of His spiritual marks appearing on *our* foreheads and right hands.

While this may seem like a lot, we may have long borne them, simply from the daily living out of our faith and, hopefully, everyone around us can see them clearly. We even teach them to children in Sunday school. After all, what Christian has not already been taught to repent, to deal with their sins as the Holy Spirit leads and convicts them? To trust in the blood of the Lamb for salvation? To love God and our neighbours? To marvel in the revelation of Jesus our Lord and our God?

'The Master of My Fate'

Having now established these marks of God's ownership, what are we to understand about all *without* them? Are they instead their own masters, as portrayed in *Invictus,* William Henley's famous 1875 poem?

> I am the master of my fate:
> I am the captain of my soul.

Invictus, Latin for unconquerable, has inspired many inspiring leaders such as South Africa's Nelson Mandela,[71] Burmese Nobel Peace laureate Aung San Suu Kyi,[72] American President Franklin D Roosevelt,[73] world tennis champion Andre Agassi[74] and singer-song writer Leonard Cohen.[75]

The whole poem reads:

> Out of the night that covers me,
> Black as the pit from pole to pole,
> I thank whatever gods may be
> For my unconquerable soul.
>
> In the fell clutch of circumstance
> I have not winced nor cried aloud.
> Under the bludgeonings of chance
> My head is bloody, but unbowed.

---

71   Eddie Daniels, *There and Back: Robben Island, 1964-1979,* Cape Town; Mayibuye Books, 1998, p. 244. Clint Eastwood's 2009 film, *Invictus,* starring Morgan Freeman and Matt Damon, has Mandela then using this poem to inspire the Springboks rugby team to beat New Zealand's All Blacks in the 1995 Rugby World Cup. Apparently, he actually quoted Theodore Roosevelt's, *The Man in the Arena.*
72   BBC Reith Lecture, 28 Jun, 2011. http://downloads.bbc.co.uk/ rmhttp/radio4/transcripts/2011_reith1.pdf, p. 5.
73   Michael R. Beschloss, *The Conquerors: Roosevelt, Truman and the Destruction of Hitler's Germany,* 1941-1945, New York, Simon and Schuster, 2002, p. 216.
74   Andre Agassi, *Open,* New York; Vintage, 2010.
75   On tour in 2010, he recited it to introduce his song, *The Darkness.*

Beyond this place of wrath and tears
Looms but the Horror of the shade,
And yet the menace of the years
Finds and shall find me unafraid.

It matters not how strait the gate,
How charged with punishments the scroll.
I am the master of my fate:
I am the captain of my soul.

Henley's admirable stoicism helped him to overcome ill health and the amputation of a leg when he was 17. His zest for life and willingness to take on all of life's challenges was the model for Robert Louis Stevenson's character Long John Silver in *Treasure Island* and his daughter inspired the character Wendy in J.M. Barrie's *Peter Pan*.

And yet there is a fatal flaw in his last verse: 'It matters not how strait the gate, how charged with punishments the scroll'.

It really *does* matter. *Invictus* also inspired Oklahoma City bomber Timothy McVeigh who killed 168 men, women and children, and wounded 450. He handed his hand-written copy to the prison warden as his final statement before his execution in 2001.[76]

The 'strait gate' is the King James Version of the 'narrow gate', as described by Jesus:

13. "Enter through the narrow gate; for the gate is wide and the way is broad that leads to destruction, and there are many who enter through it.
14. "For the gate is small and the way is narrow that leads to life, and there are few who find it." (Matt 7:13-14, *NASB*)

There are only two gates and two ways available to each of us. Henley is surely right that it is up to each one of us to choose, but Jesus calls us all to leave the wide and broad way, because it leads to destruction. Instead, He urges us to choose

---

76 www.guardian.co.uk/world/2001/jun/11/mcveigh.usa1, 4 Jul, 2013.

the 'strait gate' and the narrow way, even though only a few of us do, because that is the only way to real and eternal life.

This is one of the profound paradoxes in Jesus' teaching:

> 25. "For whoever wishes to save his life will lose it; but whoever loses his life for My sake will find it.
> 26. "For what will it profit a man if he gains the whole world and forfeits his soul? Or what will a man give in exchange for his soul?" (Matt 16:25-26)

We *must choose* to allow God to become the Master and the Captain of our souls. The only other option is to remain separated from God...:

> ...in [our] trespasses and sins, in which [we walk] according to the course of this world, according to the prince of the power of the air, of the spirit that is now working in the sons of disobedience. (Eph 2:1-2)

Being disobedient to God means we are placing ourselves under another spiritual power, Satan, who is prince over all who act as he does in disobeying God. There is no other option.

Let us now consider Satan's counterpart of each mark, one of which is the mark of the beast.

7

The Marks of Satan
Bearing His Name

Those bearing God's ownership marks belong to Him but those without them belong to 'the great dragon…, the serpent of old who is called the devil and Satan, who deceives the whole world' (Rev 12:9).

Let us ensure we know exactly how Satan's marks work. We will then identify the mark of his agent, the first beast of Revelation 13, which we established in Book 2 to be the State gone feral. It is this mark which the second beast, i.e. the spirit of antichrist, gives to 'the small and the great, and the rich and the poor, and the free men and the slaves' (Rev 13:16).

Since Satan also "disguises himself as an angel of light" and his servants "as servants of righteousness" (2 Cor 11:14-15), we can be sure his marks may appear innocuous and even very attractive.

His marks on anyone begin with *non-participation*, our refusing to accept the vicarious death of Jesus of Nazareth. From the time that He came as the ultimate Passover Lamb, dying for the sins of the whole world, the whole human race became accountable for either accepting or rejecting Him, for partaking of His sacrifice or not:

> 11. God has given us eternal life, and this life is in His Son.
> 12. He who has the Son has the life; he who does not have the Son of God does not have the life. (1 John 5:11-12)

There is quite simply no other option: we either have the Son, and thus eternal life, or we do not.

The six marks of Satan are therefore:

(i) Refusing to believe

Whereas God's first ownership mark is 'the blood of the Lamb', seen in the death of Jesus on the cross 2,000 years ago, Satan's first mark is simply our *refusing to accept* that Jesus came and died for us, as our Passover sacrifice:

> The one who does not believe God has made Him a liar, because he has not believed in the testimony that God has given concerning His Son. (1 John 5:10)

(ii) Refusing to respond

God then required the Jews to eat their Passover lamb, i.e. to accept it into their innermost being, and Jesus equated that to us metaphorically eating His flesh. Satan's second mark is therefore our *refusing to respond* to Jesus:

> 11. He came to His own [the nation of Israel], and those who were His own did not receive Him.
> 12. But as many as received Him, to them He gave the right to become children of God, even to those who believe in His name. (John 1:11-12)

(iii) Partaking of the 'leaven'

God requires every one of us to keep the metaphorical Feast of Unleavened Bread by living a loving and righteous lifestyle; the third mark of Satan's ownership is our instead *partaking of 'the leaven of malice and wickedness'*. As John puts it:

> By this the children of God and the children of the devil are obvious: anyone who does not practice righteousness is not of God, nor the one who does not love his brother. (1 John 3:10)

Of course, God does not expect perfection of us, His very fallible followers. This is why we all need to trust in Him instead of in our own goodness or works. However, He does expect us to walk in the light, which includes our seeking and receiving forgiveness for every failure:

Gotta Serve Somebody

5. This is the message we have heard from Him and announce to you, that God is Light, and in Him there is no darkness at all.
6. If we say that we have fellowship with Him and yet walk in the darkness, we lie and do not practice the truth;
7. but if we walk in the light as He Himself is in the light, we have fellowship with one another, and the blood of Jesus His Son cleanses us from all sin.
8. If we say that we have no sin, we are deceiving ourselves and the truth is not in us.
9. If we confess our sins, He is faithful and righteous to forgive us our sins and to cleanse us from all unrighteousness.
(1 John 1:5-9)

(iv) Refusing to honour Jesus

God required Israel to always honour the firstborn; the fourth mark of Satan is therefore refusing to *honour God's first-born Son.* Instead of harbouring our own ideas about Jesus, we are called to find out His true identity, to accept and trust the testimony of the Father and the Holy Spirit:

16. After being baptized, Jesus came up immediately from the water; and behold, the heavens were opened, and he saw the Spirit of God descending as a dove and lighting on Him,
17. and behold, a voice out of the heavens said, "This is My beloved Son, in whom I am well-pleased." (Matt 3:16-17)

He is who He is:

23. And He was saying to them, "You are from below, I am from above; you are of this world, I am not of this world.
24. "Therefore I said to you that you will die in your sins; for unless you believe that I am, you will die in your sins."
(John 8:23-24)

(v) Refusing to love and obey God

The greatest commandment is to wholeheartedly love and

serve Him; the fifth mark of Satan is therefore our being *unwilling to love God and to do His will*:

> 15. Do not love the world nor the things in the world. If anyone loves the world, the love of the Father is not in him.
> 16. For all that is in the world, the lust of the flesh and the lust of the eyes and the boastful pride of life, is not from the Father, but is from the world.
> 17. The world is passing away, and also its lusts; but the one who does the will of God lives forever. (1John 2:15-17)

(vi) Following false prophets

God tested Israel's loyalty by allowing false prophets to arise to lead them into idolatry; Satan's sixth mark is therefore *the acceptance of idolatry* and, in particular, *of any false prophet.*

This is why there are so many warnings in the New Testament about false prophets.[77] Consider Jesus' famous 'end of the age' discourse in Matthew 24:

> 4. "See to it that no one misleads you.
> 5. "For many will come in My name, saying, 'I am the Christ,' and will mislead many…"
>
> 11. "Many false prophets will arise and will mislead many…"
>
> 24. "For false Christs and false prophets will arise and will show great signs and wonders, so as to mislead, if possible, even the elect."

This idolatry includes a willingness to accept almost anyone else in His place:

> "I have come in My Father's name, and you do not receive Me; if another comes in his own name, you will receive him"
> (John 5:43)

As we saw in *Slouching Towards Bethlehem*, it is particularly seen in every deification and worship of a political or religious leader.

---

77   e.g. Matthew 7:15, 2 Peter 2:1, 1 John 4:1.

It is therefore this sixth mark to which John is referring in Revelation 13, when everyone in John's original audience was being required to worship the Roman emperor.

Worshipping the Emperor

At this point, we need to recall what we also established in *Slouching Towards Bethlehem* regarding the two beasts and emperor-worship.[78]

We saw that the word worship comes from 'worthship' and, in the Biblical use of the word, it means to accord ultimate worth or value. As Jesus says:

> "No one can serve two masters; for either he will hate the one and love the other, or he will be devoted to one and despise the other. You cannot serve God and wealth [lit. mammon]" (Matt 6:24)

Obviously, we do not bow down before mammon or wealth as our Creator but whoever or whatever we choose to *serve or obey* is the one we most love or value. We thereby reveal our real master.

This worship of mammon is not usually overt but for 1st Century Romans, worship of their emperors was blatant. When John was writing in 95-96 A.D., of the seven cities to which he wrote…:

> Pergamum was the regional centre of the cult… Ephesus and Smyrna competed with each other in paying such honours at festivals… Thyatira worshipped the emperor as Apollo incarnate and the son of Zeus. In 26 A.D., Sardis was among the ten cities competing for the right to build a temple in honour of the emperor but lost to Smyrna. Since Laodicea was the wealthiest city in Phrygia and especially prosperous under the Flavian emperors [including Domitian], we would certainly expect some

---

78 pp. 95-98.

form of emperor cult to be propagated [there].[79]

John's vision in Revelation 13 was to show the demonic inspiration behind this phenomenon: the second beast (the spirit of antichrist) was causing the people to worship both the first beast (at that time, Rome) and the image of that beast (the emperor).

'Full of Blasphemous Names'

Domitian was emperor when John was writing and when he ascended the throne in 81 A.D., he was inspired to name himself "Lord and God":

> …he began as follows in issuing a circular letter in the name of his procurators, "Our *dominus et deus* [our Lord and God] bids that this be done." And so the custom arose of henceforth addressing him in no other way even in writing or in conversation.[80]

The choice for John's original audience was therefore stark: either they affirmed, "Caesar is Lord!", meaning God, or they were persecuted, reviled as traitors, exiled or executed for instead saying, "Jesus is Lord!"

Some modern scholars have doubted this, claiming that Roman title 'Lord' came later. However, Adolph Deissman established that despite Augustus (27 B.C.-14 A.D.) and Tiberius (12-37 A.D.)[81] scorning the title of 'Lord' because it directly contradicted the Roman conception of the empire as a 'principate' rather than a 'dominate', they were both called Lord in Egypt and Syria before 29 A.D. So too were Caligula (37-41 A.D.) and Claudius (41-54 A.D.). Nero, who put Paul and Peter to death, was everywhere called Lord (e.g. Acts 25:26) as

---

79   Pheme Perkins, *Reading the New Testament*, 2nd Edition, New York; Paulist Press, 1988, p. 324.
80   Suetonius, *Life of Domitian*, 13:2.
81   Tiberius was co-equal with Augustus for two years. www.roman-britain.org/people/tiberius.htm, 24 Jul, 2013.

was Vespasian (69-79 A.D.).[82]

Jews and Jewish Christians readily understood the extent of the blasphemy in Greek because 'Lord' (Greek, *Kurios*) was used in the Septuagint to translate the Jews' sacred name of God, YHWH.[83] Referred to as *HaShem,* i.e. The Name (e.g. Leviticus 24:11), they considered it so holy that they instead used *Adonai,* or Lord.[84] This in turn led to our Bible translators' convention today of translating YHWH as LORD, except where it is compounded with *Adonai* when it becomes "LORD God".[85]

Accordingly, to the Jews and Jewish Christians, the Romans calling Caesar 'Lord' was plainly blasphemous and they were willing to die rather than use the title.

The Jewish Exemption

The Jews, however, were initially exempted:

> Emperor worship first appeared in Palestine during the reign of Herod the Great [37- 4 B.C.]. Although it was completely unacceptable to the Jewish population, Herod could nevertheless not afford to lag behind other vassal princes in establishing the cult. Thus although a temple was not erected in Jerusalem to honor the emperor, these rites were adopted in the cities of Sebaste and Caesarea, both predominantly non-Jewish.
>
> The Jewish population, though not the Christian, was everywhere exempted from the loyal duty of emperor

---

82   Adolph Deissman, *Light from the Ancient East*, pp. 350-356.

83   Used 5,989 times in the Hebrew Bible, these four letters are also called the Tetragrammaton. www.jewishencyclopedia.com/articles/14346-tetragrammaton, 3 Jun, 2013.

84   Literally, 'my Lords', but, like the plural *Elohim,* used with singular verbs. The plural name is held to signify respect or Pluralis Majestatis, the royal 'we'. www.hebrew4christians.com/Names_of_G-d/Adonai/adonai.html, 3 Jun, 2013. See also www.jewishencyclopedia.com/articles/840-adonai.

85   In the Masoretic Text, the Masoretes pointed to vowels which led to the pronunciation of *Ye-Ho-Vah,* hence today's Jehovah.

---

worship and only one attempt was made to compel the Jewish nation to accept emperor worship, when Caligula issued a decree to erect a statue of himself in the sanctuary at Jerusalem (Jos., Ant., 18:262; Jos., Wars, 2:184; Philo, De Legatione ad Gaium, 188, 207–8; Tacitus, Historiae, 5:9). The decree was never carried out, however, due to the death of Caligula in January 41 C.E.[86]

James Jeffers explains why they were exempt:

> In 161 B.C., the Jewish leader, Judas Maccabee, requested Roman protection from the ravages of Seleucid monarch, Antiocus IV. Wanting to weaken the Seleucids, Rome agreed to a declaration of friendship with Judea. In the following century, the Jews gave both Julius Caesar and Octavian valuable military assistance. This led to a series of official edicts and letters to Greek cities in the East, instructing them to permit resident Jews to observe their traditional religion… Even more important, they would not be required to participate in emperor worship. These privileges were not altered until after the destruction of the temple in Jerusalem in 70 A.D…[87]
>
> The Romans at first considered Christianity a sect of Judaism, and so ignored it. But by the 60s A.D., Rome began to recognize the difference…[88]

After the great fire of Rome in 64 A.D., Nero seized the opportunity to blame the Christians and, as we saw from Tacitus' graphic descriptions,[89] began a fierce persecution which led to the deaths of the apostles Peter and Paul.

The Christians made good victims because, unlike most

---

86 www.jewishvirtuallibrary.org/jsource/judaica/ejud_0002_0006_0_05937.html, 26 Feb, 2013.
87   James S. Jeffers, *The Greco-Roman World of the New Testament Era - Exploring the Background of Early Christianity,* Downers Grove, Illinois; IVP Academic, 1999, p. 105.
88   *ibid,* pp. 107-108.
89   *Slouching Towards Bethlehem,* pp. 58-59.

                                    Gotta Serve Somebody

religious groups, they totally rejected the gods of Rome. Of course, the Jews too rejected other gods, but the Jews were a known commodity; the Christians were a mysterious combination of Jews, Greeks and Romans. They acted like a single people, even though they represented many nations. To the Romans, this was clearly unnatural.[90]

In 70 A.D., however, it all changed for the Jews too. As we saw in Book 2, Titus's legions brought emperor worship into the heart of Jerusalem, into the ruins of the Temple.[91]

'He Causes All…'

Returning now to Revelation 13, we see John describing *who* is marked by the second beast, i.e. the spirit of antichrist, with the mark of the first beast, i.e. the feral state:

> 7. It was also given to him [i.e. the first beast] to make war with the saints and to overcome them, and authority over *every* tribe and people and tongue and nation was given to him.
> 8. *All* who dwell on the earth will worship him…
>
> 12. And he [i.e. the second beast] makes the earth and those who dwell in it to worship the first beast…
>
> 14. And he deceives those who dwell on the earth…
>
> 16. And *he causes all*, the small and the great, and the rich and the poor, and the free men and the slaves, *to be given a mark* on their right hand, or on their forehead… [emphasis added]

The beast's mark, Satan's sixth, is for all 'who dwell on the earth' (v. 14): 'the small and the great', i.e. regardless of their status; 'and the rich and the poor', i.e. regardless of their income'; 'and the free men and the slaves', i.e. regardless of

---

90   Jeffers, pp. 107-108.
91   *Slouching Towards Bethlehem*, pp. 205 and 278.

their citizenship (v. 16).

It is this all-inclusive characteristic that has always left me deeply dissatisfied with today's most popular interpretation of the mark of the beast as a literal mark and the basis of a new, future, monetary system. That requires us to await the creation of this system to include not only us in the West, the USA and Europe, and Russia in the East, but also the multitudes of China, India, Asia, Africa and South America.

If, however, the mark is a counterpart of one of six spiritual marks, *it already exists* in all these places and has done for two thousand years, *wherever and whenever an emperor is being worshipped.*

This is consistent with the beast's reign being for 'forty-two months' (Rev 13:5), i.e. "the times of the Gentiles" which also is the last two thousand years.[92] We are not supposed to wait for this mark but to recognise it wherever it occurs today.

'The Whole World'?

John told the 1st Century church:

> The whole world lies in the power of the evil one. (1 John 5:19)

He is not saying 'the whole world *will*', i.e. in the future, but that it *already* lies in Satan's power.

In John chapter 8, Jesus likewise warned all of His own countrymen (John 8:22, 31 and 48) and particularly the Pharisees (John 8:13) who, incidentally, may well have been wearing phylacteries:

> 42. …"If God were your Father, you would love Me, for I proceeded forth and have come from God, for I have not even come on My own initiative, but He sent Me.

In other words, if they were truly godly, they would have recognised Him. He then explained:

---

92 *Dancing in the Dragon's Jaws*, pp. 119-123.

We either belong to God or we belong to the devil (v. 44) and we do not enjoy hearing that (v. 45). Can any of us find any personal fault in Jesus (v. 46)? Since He clearly demonstrated His love for all, even the outcasts and despised minorities, as well as showing no partiality to any (Matt 22:16), we should listen to what He says:

If we belong to God, we will listen to Him; if we do not, we will not (v. 47).

Everyone in 'the whole world' is already marked as Satan's, not because he has bought them but because they are buying his lies – all of these marks are voluntary. Everyone, that is, except for those with the mark of God and, as we have yet to consider, the 144,000 of Revelation 7 and 14.

How should we respond? We are to help all who are still 'in the world' to instead be 'in Christ' or, in other words, to swap marks. Satan is right now either coercing or seducing the whole world to *keep* his marks, i.e. to refuse the sacrifice of Jesus as the Lamb and God's firstborn, to choose to remain in wickedness, to remain unloving and disobedient to God and to accept the spirit of antichrist. We are to persuade them to instead trust and love Jesus, and help them to properly deal with their attitudes and reject the spirit of antichrist.

Refusing Satan's Sixth Mark

The consequences of refusing this mark in John's day were often fatal:

> And it was given to him to give breath to the image of the beast, so that the image of the beast would even speak and cause as many as do not worship the image of the beast to be killed. (Rev 13:15)

As we saw in Book 2, *Slouching Towards Bethlehem,* the living 'image of the beast' was the emperor. In John's time, non-worship of successive emperors was a capital offence, especially when Jesus was worshipped instead. For example, in 64-65 A.D. the emperor Nero…:

> …inflicted the most exquisite tortures on a class hated for their abominations, called Christians by the populace. Christus, from whom the name had its origin, suffered the extreme penalty during the reign of Tiberius at the hands of one of our procurators, Pontius Pilatus, and a most mischievous superstition, thus checked for the moment, again broke out not only in Judaea, the first source of the evil, but even in Rome, where all things hideous and shameful from every part of the world find their centre and become popular. Accordingly, an arrest was first made of all who pleaded guilty; then, upon their information, an immense multitude was convicted… of hatred against mankind.[93]

It was during this time that both Paul and Peter were executed in Rome.

In 112 A.D., Pliny Secundus, governor of Bithynia (today's northwest Turkey), wrote a report to the Emperor Trajan:

> I interrogated them whether they were Christians; if they confessed it I repeated the question twice again, adding the threat of capital punishment; if they still persevered,

---

93 Cornelius Tacitus, *Annals,* XV.44, www.earlychristianwritings.com/tacitus.html, 26 Apr, 2008.

Gotta Serve Somebody

I ordered them to be executed. For, whatever the nature
of their creed might be, I could at least feel no doubt
that contumacy [94] and inflexible obstinacy deserved
chastisement...

Those who denied they were, or had ever been, Christians,
who repeated after me an invocation to the gods, and
offered adoration with wine and frankincense to your
image, which I had ordered to be brought for that
purpose, together with those of the gods, and who finally
cursed Christ, none of which acts, it is said, those who are
really Christians can be forced into performing, these I
thought it proper to discharge.[95]

John's condemnation of these officials and those submitting
to their idolatry is severe:

If anyone worships the beast and his image, and receives a mark
on his forehead or upon his hand, he also will drink of the wine
of the wrath of God…

And the smoke of their torment goes up forever and ever; and
they have no rest day and night, those who worship the beast
and his image, or whoever receives the mark of his name.
(Rev 14:9-11)

We see, therefore, that Jesus' earlier warnings were not poetic
or dramatic but deeply practical:

"Do not fear those who kill the body but are unable to kill the
soul; but rather fear Him who is able to destroy both soul and
body in hell" (Matt 10:28)

"I say to you, My friends, do not be afraid of those who kill the
body and after that have no more that they can do. But I will
warn you whom to fear: fear the One who, after He has killed, has
authority to cast into hell; yes, I tell you, fear Him!" (Luke 12:4-5)

---

94   i.e. insubordination or wilful disobedience.
95   *Epistles*, X. 96, www.textexcavation.com/plinytestimonium.html, 26
Apr, 2008.

In the 20th Century, Alexander Solzhenitsyn spoke similarly after eleven years of torture, imprisonment and exile in Siberia for refusing to kowtow to his Marxist emperor, Joseph Stalin:

> So what is the answer? How can you stand your ground when you are weak and sensitive to pain, when people you love are still alive, when you are unprepared? What do you need to make you stronger than your interrogator, yes, and even stronger than the whole trap?
>
> From the moment you go to prison, you must put your cozy past firmly behind you. At the very threshold, you must say to yourself: "My life is over, a little early to be sure, but there's nothing to be done about it. I shall never return to freedom. I am condemned to die - now or a little later. But later on, in truth, it will be harder, and so the sooner the better. I no longer have any property whatsoever. For me, those I love have died, and for them, I have died. From today on, my body is useless and alien to me. Only my spirit and my conscience remain precious and important to me".
>
> Confronted by such a prisoner, the interrogator will tremble. Only the man who has renounced everything can win the victory over the trap.[96]

While Solzenhitsyn was ultimately released and vindicated in 1956, John saw a different outcome but extraordinary reward for those refusing in his day:

> 2. And I saw something like a sea of glass mixed with fire, and those who had been victorious over the beast and his image and the number of his name, standing on the sea of glass, holding harps of God.
> 3. And they sang the song of Moses, the bond-servant of God,

---

96 *The Gulag Archipelago 1918-1956,* Vol One, New York; Harper & Row, 1973, p. 64. Solzhenistsyn was imprisoned in 1945 for criticising Stalin but became a Christian there through the last words of Dr. Boris Kornfeld, a doctor who treated him in a prison hospital, as described in Vol Two, 1975, p. 612 ff.

and the song of the Lamb, saying, "Great and marvelous are Your works, O Lord God, the Almighty; Righteous and true are Your ways, King of the nations!" (Rev 15:1-3)

Their families and friends may even have seen them killed but they are 'victorious over the beast and his image and the number of his name' (v. 2) because here they are, standing again, worshipping God and reigning with Him:

4. Then I saw thrones… And I saw the souls of those who… had not worshiped the beast or his image, and had not received the mark on their forehead and on their hand; and they came to life and reigned with Christ for a thousand years. (Rev 20:4)

We will consider the thousand year reign in the last book in this series.

The Nuremberg Defence

Another 20th Century illustration of our need to refuse to worship an emperor can be seen in Germany's Nuremberg Trials. After World War II, the surviving Nazi leaders tried to excuse their participation in war crimes by claiming they were only following Hitler's orders and were therefore not personally responsible. This defence, known as Superior Orders, had been successfully used after World War I by a U-Boat captain who had sunk a hospital ship. Germany's highest court had acquitted him, and many others, on the basis that:

… all civilized nations recognize the principle that a subordinate is covered by the orders of his superiors.[97]

This was considered so outrageous by the Allies, in August 1945 they issued the Nuremberg Charter in which Principle IV states:

The fact that a person acted pursuant to order of his

---

97   G.A. Finch, *Superior Orders and War Crimes, The American Journal of International Law,* Vol. 15, No. 3; 1921, pp. 440-445.

> Government or of a superior does not relieve him from
> responsibility under international law, provided a moral
> choice was in fact possible to him.

In other words, moral law is higher than national law.

This effectively ruled out what became known as the Nuremberg Defence of these leaders and later, in 1961, of Adolf Eichmann in Israel. It also became a founding principle of today's war crimes tribunal, the International Criminal Court, in The Hague.[98]

These international jurists recognise the limits of all political leadership. Even the emperor is subject to moral law — *there is simply no excuse for worshipping the beast and receiving his mark instead of God's.*

Kurt Gerstein was a radical Christian who went undercover in order to subvert Hitler's program and became an Obersturmführer in the dreaded *Schutzstaffel*, or SS. In October 1938, he wrote to his family:

> Is Germany to believe that justice is a transcendent
> concept over which the human will has no power -
> 'residing among the stars' in Schiller's phrase - and that he
> who talks of justice does so in the name of an all-powerful
> Supreme Judge to whom he is responsible? Or are we to
> concede that 'the law is whatever serves the people' - that
> is to say, a purely utilitarian affair? Is Justice to be the
> harlot of the State?[99]

Gerstein rightly saw that every citizen, especially judges, must always put their obedience to God before their obedience to the State.

While we today are not facing such extremes as the Christians in Roman times or in Hitler's Germany, any time an antichrist regime becomes dominant, this choice will always

---

98 http://untreaty.un.org/ilc/texts/instruments/english/draft%20 articles/7_1_1950.pdf, 10 Oct, 2011.
99 Gerstein's extraordinary story is told on www.auschwitz.dk/gerstein. htm, 10 Oct, 2011.

Gotta Serve Somebody

ultimately emerge. For many, it may not be in the political realm at all but, as I argued in *Slouching Towards Bethlehem*, it may be in the spiritual realm, where we are being asked to accept the teachings or commands of priests, prophets, gurus, pastors, preachers or teachers, rather than the words of Jesus.

8

'... Able to Buy or Sell'
and Much More

What then are we to make of the apparent reference to the beast's mark as the sole means of buying and selling?

> ... he provides that no one should be able to buy or sell, except the one who has the mark (Rev 13:17)

We have often been told this means that the final Antichrist will control all buying and selling, either by controlling all the world's currencies or by setting up a new global monetary system, usually as the answer to the latest financial crisis. However, trading has never been restricted to any monetary system because it includes bartering, i.e. the direct exchange of one commodity for another. Accordingly, no monetary system can ever control all 'buying and selling'.

To what then is the Scripture referring?

In the ancient world, trading was usually regulated by trade guilds, whether in Egypt, Assyria, Babylon, Greece, Rome, Syria, Persia or in Israel. These were associations of men in the same craft or trade, set up for mutual protection and for social and religious benefits.

> In Rome, as early as the 7th century B.C., there were guilds of flute players, goldsmiths, coppersmiths, fullers, shoemakers, dyers and carpenters. By the 2nd century B.C., cooks, tanners, builders, bronze workers, iron workers, weavers, and priests all had their own guilds and membership in a guild was compulsory. No one was permitted to leave the guild in which he was enrolled, and a son was required to follow the trade of his father. In Assyria, people were divided into five classes, with the patricians or nobles at the top, and craftsmen and

Gotta Serve Somebody

professions organised into guilds directly below them. In Persia, there was a well-organised guild of physicians and surgeons whose fees were fixed by law.[100]

Remember, this is the day-to-day world of John's original audience in the seven churches of Asia Minor. It was the same in the land of Israel:

> It was the custom for tradesmen in larger cities in the Near East to live in separate quarters. For example, Jerusalem had a bakers' street (Jeremiah 37:21) and a goldsmiths' district (Nehemiah 3:32)… In the post-exilic period, guilds were powerful organisations and were recognised by the government. A guild could prevent a craftsman from another area from working in its territory. It had a trade monopoly in its particular locality. A guild could monopolise the market. Guild members were insured against loss of tools, animals and boats used in their business… (and they) had their own religious and social institutions, even their own synagogues [e.g. Acts 6:9], next to which there were burial grounds for the members.[101]

This control of buying and selling has nothing to do with a particular currency and everything to do with commercial and political association. In a particularly horrifying modern example, between 1958 and 1962 Mao Zedong exported most of China's food to fund his nuclear ambitions, cold-bloodedly starving some forty-three million of his fellow citizens. He gave the benefit of his reasoning to a meeting in Shanghai on 25 March, 1959:

> When there is not enough to eat, people starve to death. It is better to let half of the people die so that the other half can eat their fill.[102]

---

100 *The Zondervan Pictorial Encyclopedia of the Bible*, Vol. 5, p. 792.
101 Ibid.
102 Frank Dikötter, *Mao's Great Famine: The History of China's Most Devastating Catastrophe, 1958-1962*, New York; Bloomsbury and Walker

Since China's first modern census in 1953 had shown a larger than expected population of 583 million,[103] perhaps Mao thought he could spare some.

Daily Life

We have also wrongly limited the effects of the mark to 'buying and selling'. Elsewhere in the Scriptures, this expression is used to describe just one aspect of many in their ordinary, daily life which would be disrupted by cataclysmic events. For example, when Jesus describes Lot's society:

> "They were eating, they were drinking, they were buying, they were selling, they were planting, they were building; but on the day…" (Luke 17:28-29)

Similarly, in His description of Noah's society:

> "They were eating, they were drinking, they were marrying, they were being given in marriage, until the day…" (Luke 17:27)

The Lord is here contrasting their normal everyday lives with the suddenness of their demise. We should therefore expect that those without the beast's mark are not just forbidden to trade ("buying and selling") but are also ostracised and excluded from many other aspects of normal society such as taking meals together ("eating and drinking"), joining families ("marrying and being given in marriage") and vocations ("planting and building").

As we saw earlier in Revelation 13:5, this is supposed to take place throughout the beast's reign of 'forty-two months' which, as argued in *Dancing in the Dragon's Jaws*, means over the last two thousand years. *This ostracism has therefore already happened* to multitudes of people as they have become Christians, removing the mark of the beast to take the mark of God.

Press, 2010. Quoted in www.nytimes.com/2010/12/16/opinion/16iht-eddikotter16.htmlp. 792, 15 Dec, 2010.

103 www.cecc.gov/pages/virtualAcad/his/prc.php, 22 Dec, 2010.

Gotta Serve Somebody

It was in about 64 A.D. that Nero declared that following Jesus was a *religio ilicita* (illegal religion) throughout the Roman Empire. Remember Cornelius Tacitus's account of what happened then, and the report of Pliny Secundus from 112 A.D. recording executions under Trajan (see 'Refusing Satan's Sixth Mark', previous chapter). Throughout the next two hundred years there were official and unofficial persecutions of Christians[104] which, when not actually murderous, still saw them shut out of normal society. In 303 A.D., during the reign of Diocletian:

> ...an imperial letter was everywhere promulgated, ... proclaiming that those who held high positions would lose all civil rights, while those in households, if they persisted in their profession of Christianity, would be deprived of their liberty.[105]

Easily identifiable because they no longer ate in pagan temples or poured out libations to emperors, the early Christians could also be sent into exile, as was John on Patmos, or have all their possessions confiscated (Heb 10:32-34).

We can see then that while the mark enables buying and selling, it is not limited to that nor is it an actual means of buying and selling.

---

104   The worst persecutions were during the reigns of Nero (64-68 A.D.), Domitian (95-96 A.D.), Trajan (112-117 A.D), Marcus Aurelius (161-180 A.D.), Septimus Severus (202-210 A.D.), Maximinus the Thracian (235-238 A.D.), Decius (249-251 A.D.), Valerian (257-260 A.D.) and co-emperors Diocletian and Galerius (303-311 A.D.). Laurie Guy, *Introducing Early Christianity*, Downers Grove, Illinois; IVP, 2004, pp. 50-73.
105   *Cambridge History of the Bible*, Cambridge University Press, 1963. p. 476.

Libelli and Charagma

During at least one period of persecution, official documents called *libelli* were issued, certifying compliance with the emperor's edicts, and accepted as proof that the bearer was not a Christian.

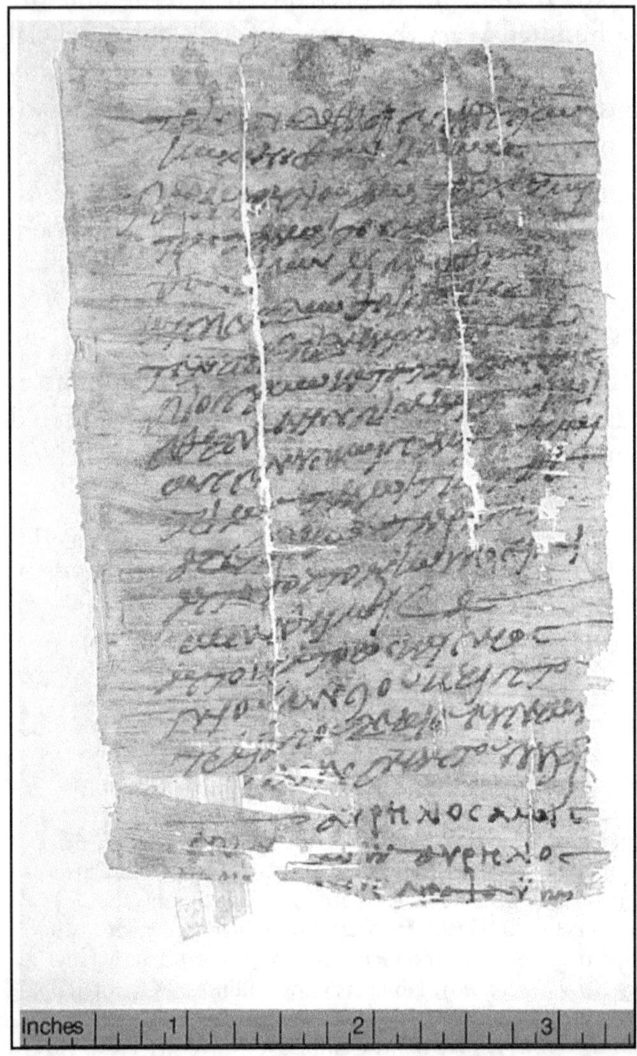

Photo (iii) A Libellus of the Decian Persecution (250 A.D.)

> Translation from Greek:
> To those in charge of the sacrifices of the village
> Theadelphia, from Aurelia Bellias, daughter of Peteres,
> and her daughter, Kapinis. We have always been constant
> in sacrificing to the gods, and now too, in your presence,
> in accordance with the regulations, I have poured
> libations and sacrificed and tasted the offerings, and I
> ask you to certify this for us below. May you continue to
> prosper.(2nd hand) We, Aurelius Serenus and Aurelius
> Hermas, saw you sacrificing.
> (3rd hand) I, Hermas, certify.
> (1st hand) The 1st year of the Emperor Caesar Gaius
> Messius Quintus Traianus Decius Pius Felix Augustus,
> Pauni 27.[106]

These official persecutions only ceased when first Galerius in 311 A.D. and then Constantine in 313 A.D. issued imperial edicts and Constantine seemed to embrace the new faith.

This concept of the mark of the beast as emperor-worship is confirmed by John using the Greek word *charagma* seven times, all in Revelation and all referring to the mark of the beast.[107] It means a stamp or impress, as graven or engraved,[108] but was also used as a technical term to describe a seal on official documents.

Adolph Deissman (1866-1937) was Professor of New Testament Exegesis at Berlin University and is best known for proving the New Testament was written in *koine* or common rather than classical Greek.

---

106 www.bible-researcher.com/persecution.html#libelli, 30 Jan, 2010.
107 Revelation 13:16 & 17, 14:9 & 11, 16:2, 19:20 and 20:4. Luke records Paul also using it once, in his Mars Hill address, to describe "an image formed by the art and thought of man" (Acts 17:29).
108 W.E.Vine, *Expository Dictionary of New Testament Words,* London; Oliphants, 1975, Vol II, p. 173 and Vol III, p. 43.

Deissman writes of John's obvious knowledge of…:

> … the custom, now known to us from the papyri, of imprinting on deeds of sale and similar documents a stamp which contained the name and regnal year of the Emperor which was called, as in the Revelation, a charagma.[109]

Photo (iv) Example of an imperial seal used in Alexandria in 5-6 A.D., now in the Berlin Museum. The letters are, of course, reversed.[110]

The seal in photo (iv) has not only the name of the emperor Augustus but also the number 35, the number of years into his reign. While this does not yet fulfill Revelation 13:18, as we will see next, it does mean that John's charagma or imperial seal did not have to wait for the 21st Century to come into existence.

John's innovation was to transfer the *literal* charagma of Roman documents to the Jewish *metaphor* of forehead and hand. It was not literally engraved into anyone's forehead or

---

109 Adolph Deissman, *Light From the Ancient East*, 1910, p. 341.
110 Adolph Deissman, *Light From the Ancient East*, 1910, plate opposite p. 341. Also www.archive.org/stream/lightfromancientoodeis#page/n483/mode/2up, 26 Jan, 2010.

Gotta Serve Somebody

hand – their 'owner's name' was readily perceived in the daily lives of those willing to pour out the libations, burn the incense and call Caesar their Lord and God.

As for today, marks of imperial favour did not end with the Roman Empire any more than emperor-worship did. As we established in Book 2, many manifestations of emperor worship dramatically erupted in the 20th Century. By the mid-point of the century, the personality cults surrounding Stalin, Hirohito, Mussolini, Hitler and Muhammad meant that these five god-emperors were concurrent while the cults of Mao, Hoxha, Ceausescu, Kim Il Sung and Pol Pot were about to emerge.

All of these totalitarian states found the control of a Christian's employment or ability to trade particularly easy, as well summarised in *Encarta 96*:

> Total subjection of the individual became possible only through advanced science and industrial technology. Among the decisive, technologically conditioned features of totalitarian dictatorships are a monopoly of mass communications, a terroristic secret-police apparatus, a monopoly of all effective weapons of destruction, and a centrally controlled economy...
>
> The centrally controlled economy enables the totalitarian dictatorship to… control the workers and make them dependent on the government. Without a work permit none can work. Work permits can be withdrawn for offences such as objecting to foul working conditions...[111]

The nearest modern equivalent of both libelli and charagma seems to be the membership papers of political regimes as in Nazi Germany, or in the USSR where the *Nomenklatura* [112]

---

111 *Totalitarianism*, 1996.
112 Communist Party members who held key positions in government, industry, education, agriculture etc. www.ucl.ac.uk/ceelbas/workshops/ international_elites_workshops/Shkaratan_Paper_Lane_Workshop.pdf, 1 Jul, 2011.

received special privileges. However, the charagma was required for all Roman subjects.

Lastly, regime membership is *not in itself* the mark of the beast which God judges (Rev 14:9-11). Rather, He judges our hearts.

> Therefore do not go on passing judgment before the time, but wait until the Lord comes who will both bring to light the things hidden in the darkness and disclose *the motives of men's hearts;* and then each man's praise will come to him from God
> (1 Cor 4:5, emphasis added)

In some remarkable instances, courageous Christians infiltrated these regimes as undercover agents in order to bring them down.[113] They will certainly not be condemned for their membership when their motives are disclosed.

Persecution and Ostracism

Modern day persecution of Christians, often at the time of their baptism, is so common that most of us will have had some experience or have heard testimonies. A close friend of mine, working behind the Iron Curtain in the 1980s, told me of the heart-break of his Russian friends when the authorities forcibly removed their children from them on the grounds that they were now 'psychologically unfit' parents because they believed in an invisible God.

On the other hand, religious societies have always exercised the power of ostracism, of forbidding marriages or refusing to eat and drink with anyone they deem heretical. A Malaysian friend of mine from a Buddhist family was completely cut off by them when he was baptised as a believer in Jesus, as have others from Hinduism, Sikhism, Islam, and from many cults within Christianity such as the Exclusive Brethren. In

---

113 For example, Kurt Gerstein in Nazi Germany. See www.auschwitz.dk/gerstein.htm, 1 Jul, 2011.

                                    Gotta Serve Somebody

1973, a close friend who had just become a Christian went home one night to her traditional Catholic family to find all her belongings on the footpath. Happily, in some of these situations, there was later reconciliation.

What then are we to make of the differing degrees of severity in these instances?

Even in Roman times, there were times when Christians were not so severely persecuted or killed.

We see then that every culture and era tolerates genuine followers of Jesus to a lesser or greater degree *as the spirit of antichrist rises up or retreats within it.* Those of us living today in the western democracies can easily not recognise that we are living in a respite from the worst excesses, protected by even the waning influence of our Judeo-Christian heritage, as described in Book 2.

Summary of Satan's Marks

The six marks of Satan's ownership are simply the corollary of six marks of God's ownership that we identified, initially from the Old Testament, as being on believing Jews, and then from the New Testament, as on genuine followers of Jesus.

We established that:

(i)   None are literal marks; all are metaphorical.

(ii)   The first two marks concerned the Passover lamb which prefigured the death of Jesus and our response to Him. The first mark of Satan's ownership is therefore *refusing to accept* that Jesus came and died in our place, while the second is *refusing to respond.*

(iii) The third mark of Satan's ownership is *partaking of 'the leaven of malice and wickedness'* instead of living a loving and righteous lifestyle.

(iv)   The fourth mark is *refusing to honour Jesus* in exactly the same way as we are supposed to honour the Father, as God incarnate.

(v) The fifth is *being unwilling to love God and to do His will.*

(vi) The sixth is *accepting any antichrist,* any false prophet in the place of Jesus. It is this sixth mark that is the infamous mark of the beast.

The mark of the beast is:

(i) Usually considered to affect only the wearer's "buying and selling". However, this phrase describes just one aspect of daily life so the mark affects much more than money; it impacts all aspects of life including socialising ("eating and drinking"), joining families ("marrying and being given in marriage") and vocations ("planting and building").

(ii) In John's time, it was an integral part of emperor-worship. Everyone was required to offer incense and a libation before an image of the emperor. All of those refusing were thereby refusing the mark of the beast and were often executed or ostracised from normal society.

(iii) This means the mark enabled buying and selling but was neither a form of currency nor any other means of trading.

(iv) The Greek word John uses, *charagma,* confirms this. It means not only an engraved image but also was a technical term for the official imperial seal placed on documents. It bore the name of the emperor and the year of his reign.

(v) John transferred the literal seal from Roman documents to the Jewish metaphor of forehead and hand to illustrate who belonged to whom when they worshipped.

(vi) While the Roman charagma is no longer around, official stamps and seals have been used in this way in the last 100 years to validate emperor-worship in Stalin's USSR, Hitler's Germany, Hirohito's Japan and all of their occupied countries. Although not being used in this literal way at the moment, the metaphor remains intact and is still manifest in the subjection required by some religious movements as well as by Islamic nations.

9

'The Number of His Name'
Today's Calculations

> 17. and he provides that no one should be able to buy or sell, except the one who has the mark, either the name of the beast or the number of his name.
> 18. Here is wisdom. Let him who has understanding calculate the number of the beast, for the number is that of a man; and his number is six hundred and sixty-six (Rev 13)

The number of ways this number is calculated today is nothing short of bewildering and despite the seriousness of the issue, often comical. As we saw earlier, many since Irenaeus in the 2nd Century have been relying on the numeric values of Greek, Hebrew, Aramaic or Latin letters. They have translated the names or titles of various political leaders such as the Roman emperors Nero, Caligula or Domitian, or more recently Oliver Cromwell, Napoleon Bonaparte and Henry Kissinger, into one of these languages and ended up with a total of 666.

Some scholars appear to be bluffing their way through. For example:

> No first century Semitic reader would have any difficulty figuring out that the number of the beast in 13:18 is the spelling of "Nero Caesar" in a semitic alphabet.[114]

---

114   Pheme Perkins, *Reading the New Testament*, New York; Paulist Press, 1988, pp. 321-322. Actually that name has to initially be in Greek with an added n, *neron kaiser*, and then transliterated into Hebrew, nrwn qsr, to become 666. If left in Greek, it is 955 or with the extra n, 1005, or in non-transliterated Hebrew, 256 or 306. In other words, it only works out in a Semitic language after it has been transliterated from Greek with an extra n! http://penelope.uchicago.edu/~grout/encyclopaedia_romana/gladiators/nero.html, 30 Jan, 2010.

This writer then confidently quotes an ancient apocalyptic text which predicted that Nero would come back to life:

> …the Jewish Sibylline Oracles [115] "…when the blazing matricidal exile [Nero] returns from the ends of the earth, he will give [all the wealth of the world] to all…"
> …For the Sibylline Oracles [the power of Rome] is to be smashed in a political victory, led by the emperor Nero returned to life…
>
> The legend of Nero redivivus is mentioned in Revelation 13:3 as the head with a "mortal wound" that heals then seduces the world. [116]

Despite such bold assertions for Revelation 13:3, this was neither John's belief nor source material. As we saw in *Slouching Towards Bethlehem,* chapter 4 'His Fatal Wound', John is referring to Genesis 3:15 from the Hebrew Scriptures which had far greater antiquity and credibility. Likewise Paul in Romans 16:20.

And what of every 'first century Semitic reader… figuring out' that Revelation 13:18 referred to Nero? Early in the 2nd Century, Irenaeus was taught by Polycarp, Bishop of Smyrna, and he had not learned it this way nor did he figure it out this way. As seen earlier, Irenaeus's best guess was that 666 might be *Lateinos* (Greek for 'Latin man') and therefore the Romans in general.

This led many to later believe that it referred to the Pope and the Roman Catholic Church's Latin Mass; I was myself taught this in 1973 and we will consider the idea soon.

In the late 4th and early 5th Century, Augustine was

---

115   Usually dated as written between the 2nd Century B.C. and 2nd Century A.D., with Book V, the one being referenced, about 80 A.D. www.preteristarchive.com/BibleStudies/JewishSources/Apocalyptic/0080_sibylline-4_apocalyptic.html, 27 Apr, 2010.
116   Ibid.

scathing in his dismissal of the supposed *Nero redivivus* connection in his commentary on 2 Thessalonians 2:7:

> Some think that the Apostle Paul…alluded to Nero, whose deeds already seemed to be as the deeds of Antichrist. And hence some suppose that he shall rise again and be Antichrist. Others, again, suppose that he is not even dead, but that he was concealed that he might be supposed to have been killed, and that he now lives in concealment in the vigor of that same age which he had reached when he was believed to have perished, and will live until he is revealed in his own time and restored to his kingdom. But I wonder that men can be so audacious in their conjectures.[117]

The Number of the Pope?

Before the *Left Behind* series, the most widely held candidate to be the Antichrist was the Papacy, i.e. the successive leaders of the Roman Catholic Church.

Most of the original Protestants believed this: John Wycliffe (1324-1384), Martin Luther (1483-1546), Thomas Cranmer (1489-1556), William Tyndale (1494-1536), John Knox (1505-1572) and John Calvin (1509-1564).

So too did Puritan leaders Roger Williams (1603-1683), George Fox (1624-1691) and Cotton Mather (1663-1728), later revivalists John Wesley (1703-1791) and Charles Finney (1792-1875), and renowned preachers Charles Spurgeon (1834-1892) and Dwight L Moody (1837-1899).

Calvin, for example, wrote in 1544 in *The Necessity of Reforming the Church*:

> I deny that See [the Roman Catholic seat of supreme authority] to be Apostolical, wherein nought is seen but a shocking apostasy - I deny him to be the Vicar of Christ, who, in furiously persecuting the gospel, demonstrates by his conduct that he is Antichrist…[118]

117　*De Civitate Dei*, XX.19.3

118　www.mountainretreatorg.net/classics/necreform4.html, 26 Feb, 2013.

　Gotta Serve Somebody

Luther wrote in 1546 *Against the Roman Papacy; an Institution of the Devil* in which he defines the pope as 'a murderer of kings and inciter of all kinds of bloodshed… an Antichrist'.[119] He explained in his table-talk:

> I believe the pope is the masked and incarnate devil because he is the Antichrist. As Christ is God incarnate, so the Antichrist is the devil incarnate… The kingdom of the pope really signifies the terrible wrath of God, namely, the abomination of desolation standing in the holy place.[120]

The famous Presbyterian creed of 1646, the Westminster Confession of Faith, is similarly specific:

> There is no other head of the church but the Lord Jesus Christ. Nor can the pope of Rome in any sense be head thereof; but is that Antichrist, that man of sin and son of perdition that exalteth himself in the church against Christ and all that is called God.[121]

Notice, they do not identify the Papacy from the number 666 but rather from the Roman Church's murderous persecution of the reformers, as we saw in Book 2, and its claims that each succeeding pontiff is *Vicarius Christi*, the Vicar of Christ or, literally, 'the one in the place of Christ'. However, Pope Francis has recently set aside this title, relegating it to an historical footnote.[122]

When I was a new Christian, in 1973, I was taught that the papal crown bears the Latin inscription *Vicarius Filii Dei (lit.* In the place of the Son of God) which I was told *adds up to 666* when calculated according to Roman numerals and setting non-Roman numerals as zero. See Figure (iii).

---

119 *Luther's Works*, Vol. 41, Minneapolis; Fortress Press, pp. 357-358.
120 *Luther's Works*, Vol. 54, Table Talks, No. 4487, Minneapolis; Fortress Press, p. 346.
121 Chapter 25, article vi.
122 www.die-tagespost.de/kirche-aktuell/aktuell/Es-war-einmal-ein-Stellvertreter-Christi;art4874,206976, 16 May, 2020.

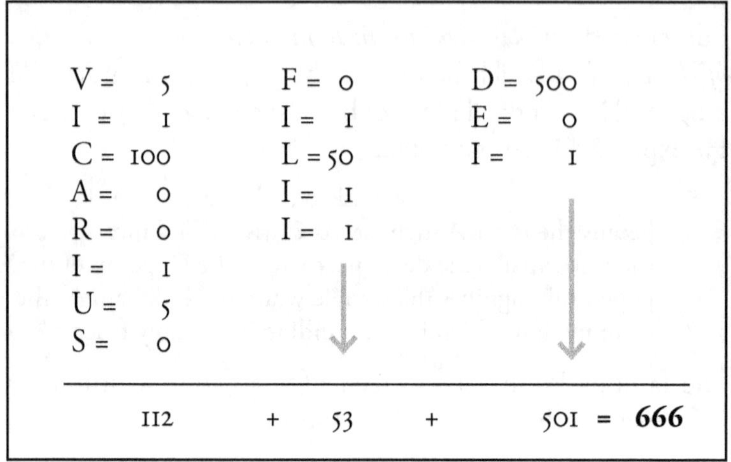

Figure (iii) 'Recalculating' the number

This 666 on his crown, I was assured, confirmed that the Pope is the Antichrist.

I recently heard this again, being taught by a Seventh Day Adventist minister, but a change in understanding is coming:

> The conclusion of recent Adventist studies, including the Sabbath School Lesson of June 1-7, 2002, is that the traditional numerical interpretation of the number 666 as representing the numerical value of the letter Vicarius Filii Dei, cannot be legitimately defended exegetically and historically.[123]

On checking for myself these many years later, I too have found that *Vicarius Filii Dei* is not an official title of the Pope nor is there any evidence of it on any crown or mitre. It seems this rumour grew from Andreas Helwig's calculations in 1612. He was a German classicist and linguist and the rector of the University of Berlin who published *Antichristus Romanus*[124] in

---

123 S. Bacchiocchi, *Our Adventist Church Has Struggled to Define 666.* ENDTIME ISSUES NEWSLETTER No. 144, Mar 15, 2006.

124 *Antichristus Romanus, in proprio suo nomine, numerum illum Apocalypticum (DCLXVI) continente proditus,* i.e. Roman Antichrist: in his own name betrayed by an Apocalyptic number (666), Wittenberg,

which he calculated fifteen *possible* titles in Hebrew, Greek, and Latin which add up to 666. These included *Vicarius Filii Dei,* Irenaeus's *Lateinos* (Greek: Latin-speaking man) as well as *He Latine Basileia* (Greek: the Latin kingdom), *Italika Ekklesia* (Greek: Italian Church) and *Dux Cleri* (Latin: Leader of the Clergy). It surely demonstrates the power of tradition that Helwig's brain-storming changed into fact in some quarters today.

Of course, this misunderstanding does not prove the Pope is *not* the Antichrist - just that his fulfilling the number 666 has not been proved.

616?

Some ancient manuscripts have the number 616 and recently, in May 2005, scholars at Oxford University found it again using new imaging techniques to read previously illegible portions of a 3rd Century papyrus.[125]

However, Irenaeus was in no doubt in the 2nd Century that John gave us the number 666. He argued from documentary evidence, oral testimony and typology, i.e. that the repetition of 6 points to what he called 'the recapitulations of apostasy' i.e. the 'summing up' of all sin against God:

> …this number being found in all the most approved and
> ancient copies [of the Apocalypse], and those men who
> saw John face to face bearing their testimony [to it]; while
> reason also leads us to conclude that the number of the
> name of the beast, [if reckoned] according to the Greek
> mode of calculation by the [value of] the letters contained
> in it, will amount to six hundred and sixty and six; that is,
> the number of tens shall be equal to that of the hundreds,
> and the number of hundreds equal to that of the units
> (for that number which [expresses] the digit six being

1612. www.archive.org/details/antichristusromanus, 30 May, 2011.
125 Papyrus 115 from Oxyrhynchus in Egypt, www.csad.ox.ac.uk/POxy/beast616.htm, 7 Dec, 2009.

---

adhered to throughout, indicates the recapitulations of
that apostasy, taken in its full extent, which occurred at
the beginning, during the intermediate periods, and which
shall take place at the end).[126]

He then explained how this error of 616 may have occurred:

I do not know how it is that some have erred following
the ordinary mode of speech, and have vitiated the middle
number in the name, deducting the amount of fifty from
it, so that instead of six decads [sic] they will have it that
there is but one. (I am inclined to think that this occurred
through the fault of the copyists, as is wont to happen,
since numbers also are expressed by letters; so that the
Greek letter which expresses the number sixty was easily
expanded into the letter iota of the Greeks.) [as we will see
next in the section, Chi Xi Stigma.] Others then received
this reading without examination; some in their simplicity,
and upon their own responsibility, making use of this
number expressing one decad [sic]; while some, in their
inexperience, have ventured to seek out a name which
should contain the erroneous and spurious number.[127]

He foresaw two very serious consequences, the first being
God's punishment on those misleading others like this, and
the second, that settling on the wrong man means we will be
easily deceived by the real one:

Moreover, another danger, by no means trifling, shall
overtake those who falsely presume that they know
the name of Antichrist. For if these men assume one
[number], when this [Antichrist] shall come having
another, they will be easily led away by him, as supposing
him not to be the expected one, who must be guarded
against.[128]

---

126 *Against Heresies*, Book V, chapter XXX, para 1, www.ccel.org/ccel/
schaff/anf01.ix.vii.xxxi.html, emphasis added, 2 Jun, 2013.
127 Ibid. Comment inserted.
128 Ibid.

                                          Gotta Serve Somebody

He concluded:

> These men, therefore, ought to learn [what really is the
> state of the case], and go back to the true number of the
> name, that they be not reckoned among false prophets.
> But, knowing the sure number declared by Scripture, that
> is, six hundred sixty and six, let them await, in the first
> place, the division of the kingdom into ten...[129]

> It is therefore more certain, and less hazardous, to await
> the fulfilment of the prophecy, than to be making
> surmises, and casting about for any names that may
> present themselves, inasmuch as many names can be
> found possessing the number mentioned; and the same
> question will, after all, remain unsolved. For if there are
> many names found possessing this number, it will be asked
> which among them shall the coming man bear. It is not
> through a want of names containing the number of that
> name that I say this, but on account of the fear of God,
> and zeal for the truth...[130]

He also reasoned that if they had needed a particular name at
that time, John would given us one:

> We will not, however, incur the risk of pronouncing
> positively as to the name of Antichrist; for if it were
> necessary that his name should be distinctly revealed in
> this present time, it would have been announced by him
> who beheld the apocalyptic vision [i.e. John]. For that
> was seen no very long time since, but almost in our day,
> towards the end of Domitian's reign [i.e. 96 A.D.].[131]

---

129 www.ccel.org/ccel/schaff/anf01.ix.vii.xxxi.html, para 2, 2 Jun, 2013.
We saw that 'the division of the kingdom into ten' in Book 2, *Slouching
Towards Bethlehem* is metaphorical rather than literal.
130 Ibid., para 3.
131 Ibid.

Chi Xi Stigma

In the two oldest extant Greek texts of Revelation 13:8,[132] John's number is not in words but in Greek letters which also serve as numbers: χ ξ ς (*chi xi stigma* – our English equivalent is cxs) where *chi* = 600, *xi* = 60 and *stigma* = 6.[133] A scribal mark above it indicates that this is an abbreviation and two other very early Greek texts[134] write out the whole number as *hexakosioi hexēkonta hex* (i.e. six hundred and sixty-six), showing how the scribes understood it.

It is therefore, as Irenaeus carefully explained, the number 6, plus its multiple by 10, plus its multiple by 100, totalling 666. In *The Bible Speaks Today* series published by Inter Varsity Press, Michael Wilcock suggests that 'this is three times falling short of the divine 7':

> Let us therefore paraphrase the verse, as it might have been read to those original hearers. "Let him who has understanding work out a number for the beast - a 'human' number, a code…" What might we suggest? "How about something which tries to look like the truth, but isn't?" "A number as close as any be to perfection, but not achieving it?" "And if the symbol of basic truth is seven, how about six for false religion?" "That would be very appropriate. Actually, perhaps because the beast in all its activities is persistently missing the mark, the number John writes here is not just 6, but 666". It may not

---

132 Chester Beatty Papyri P47 (3rd Century) and the Codex Vaticanus No. 1209 (4th Century).

133 This now obsolete character, *stigma*, is today often called *episēmon* and is not to be confused with *sigma*, the 18th letter in the Greek alphabet which corresponds to the number 200. *Stigma*, also called *digamma* or *wau*, represented the letter w and the number 6 but is today only used for 6. The noun *stigma* means a mark, dot, puncture or sign, from the verb, to puncture.

134 The Codex Sinaiticus (4th Century) – which can seen on-line at www.codex-sinaiticus.net/en/manuscript.aspx?book=59&chapter=13&lid=en&side=r&verse=18&zoomSlider=0, accessed 2 Jun, 2013 – and Codex Alexandrinus (5th Century).

have been exactly like that. But such an approach seems consistent with Revelation's general use of symbolism…[135]

A very different approach has been taken by Walid Shoebat and Simon Altaf, based not on the meaning of *chi xi stigma* but on the *shape* of these three Greek letters. Walid was born a Palestinian Muslim and Simon, an Iranian Muslim with a Jewish ancestry (both are now Christians) and they point out that the first two letters look like two Arabic letters.[136] Then, along with co-writer Joel Richardson, a Messianic Jew, Walid asks:

> Could it be possible that certain scribes viewed what were thought to be three Greek letters (Chi Xi Stigma), when in reality these were three squiggles or foreign symbols?… As soon as I began to examine the Codex Vaticanus (350 A.D.) Greek text…, I immediately noticed that the supposed Greek letters (Chi Xi Stigma) that are used to translate to the number 666 very much resemble the most common creed of Islam, Bismallah (or Basmalah), written in Arabic. Bismallah literally means "in the Name of Allah", and is followed by the symbol of crossed swords, which is used universally throughout the Muslim world to signify Islam.[137]

> In light of this, is it possible that the apostle John, while receiving his divine revelation, did not see Greek letters, but instead was supernaturally shown Arabic words and an Islamic symbol, which he then faithfully recorded? Could it be that years after John recorded these images, scribes commissioned to copy the text were unable to recognize the foreign words and symbols and thus thought them to be Greek letters?[138]

---

135 Michael Wilcock, *The Message of Revelation*, Leicester; IVP, 1975, p. 131.
136 *This is Our Eden, This is Our End*. Abrahamic Faith Ministries, 2004.
137 *God's War on Terror (Islam, Prophecy and the Bible)*, Top Executive Media, 2008, p. 369.
138 Ibid., p. 371.

Walid notes that Muslim militants routinely tie bands around their foreheads and right arms with the Islamic creed, "No God but Allah, and Muhammad is His messenger", and thus are marking themselves.[139] His strongest evidence is the Islamic prophecy of a coming beast, *Dabat Al-Ard* (lit. the Beast out of the Earth), like John's second beast of Revelation 13, but which the Qur'an says is *good*. Walid quotes the Qur'an and a hadith[140] and then explains:

> "We [Allah] shall bring forth a Beast of the Earth to speak unto them because mankind had not faith in Our revelations [to Muhammad]" (Qur'an 27:82)… [The hadith explains:] "The task of the Beast will be to distinguish the believers from the non-believers; with Prophet Moses's staff, it (the Beast) will draw a line on the forehead of every [Muslim] believer whereby his face will become bright and luminous and with the ring of Solomon, it will seal the nose of every non-believer whereby his whole face will become black. Thus there will be complete distinction between the Muslim and non-Muslim"… Can you imagine my shock when I studied the Bible? I was taught that a Beast would come "out of the earth" and he would mark the foreheads of all true Muslims… As a Muslim, I wanted the Mark of the Beast! Not surprisingly, according to Islamic tradition, this Beast comes out of Mecca.[141]

What should we make of Walid's points?

Firstly, he is right regarding the beast 'out of the earth' because, as we established in *Slouching Towards Bethlehem*, John's second beast, in Revelation 13:11, is the spirit of antichrist. We also saw that Muhammad was a living image of John's first beast, i.e. the State gone feral, just like John's 1st Century Roman emperors and the 20th Century's Stalin,

---

139   Ibid., p. 377.

140   Hadiths are traditions not found in the Qur'an but considered authoritative.

141   Ibid., p. 377-378, explanations added.

                                                    Gotta Serve Somebody

Hirohito, Mussolini, Hitler, Mao, Pol Pot et al. Accordingly, Walid's conclusion regarding Islam and Muhammad is correct.

However, he and Simon Altaf are wrong in reading this into *chi xi stigma*. It is not good exegesis to have to assume so much, i.e. that John was 'supernaturally shown Arabic words and an Islamic symbol' which could not have any relevance at all to his audience for at least another five hundred years and seemingly incomprehensible for the last nineteen hundred.

Instead, we know the word that John used, charagma, was used in the 1st Century as a technical term to describe the seal of the emperors. It can, of course, be applied to Muhammad's control of his subjects, as it can be to that of all antichrists, but it is not limited to him or to any one of them.

Rather than giving up on the significance of the number as a number, we actually need to dig a little deeper, just as we found we had to with the marks of God.

Other Guesses

Some try using the English language and beginning with a=100, b=101, c=102 etc., they then show that Hitler = 666. Quite why we should start with 100 is not explained and, using this calculation, people named Aubrey, Dwayne and Judith should also be watched carefully!

Then there is triangulation in which any number of dots that forms a perfect triangle is identified as a triangular number (e.g. 3, 6, 10, 15 etc). By this astonishing method, Barack Obama is identified as the Antichrist.[142]

One of my favourite guesses is in Leo Tolstoy's epic novel *War and Peace,* which also documents how many in 19th Century Russia understood the mark. Tolstoy's hero, Count Pyotr Bezukhov, becomes convinced from his calculations that he is predestined to assassinate the French emperor Napoleon.

---

142   For example, www.fivedoves.com/rapture/2009/Obama_Rev1318. html, 13 Feb, 2013.

He first learns from the Freemasons that:

> The French alphabet, written out with the same numerical values as the Hebrew, in which the first nine letters denote units and the others tens [i.e. a=1, b=2…i=9, k=10, l=20… z=160], will have the following significance…Writing the words L'Empereur Napoleon in numbers, it appears that the sum of them is 666, and that Napoleon therefore the beast foretold in the Apocalypse. Moreover, by applying the same system to the words quarante-deux [French, 42] which was the term allowed to the beast that "spoke great things and blasphemies," the same number 666 was obtained; from which it followed that the limit fixed for Napoleon's power had come in the year 1812 when the French emperor was forty-two.

> This prophecy pleased Pierre very much and he often asked himself what would put an end to the power of the beast, that is, of Napoleon, and tried by the same system of using letters as numbers and adding them up, to find an answer... Once when making such calculations he wrote down his own name in French, Comte Pierre Besouhoff, but the sum of the numbers did not come right. Then he changed the spelling…, [added in] his nationality… [and] wrote Le russe Besuhof and adding up the numbers got 671. This was only five too much… By omitting the e, though incorrectly, Pierre got the answer he sought. L'russe Besuhof made 666.

> …he was L'russe Besuhof who had the number of the beast, 666; that his part in the great affair of setting a limit to the power of the beast that spoke great and blasphemous things had been predestined from eternity, and that therefore he ought not to undertake anything, but wait for what was bound to come to pass.[143]

To obtain 666, the Freemasons and the Count first transpose

---

143 Leo Tolstoy, *War and Peace*, Book 9 - 1812, Chapter XIX; http://tolstoy.thefreelibrary.com/War-and-Peace/9-19, 14 Dec, 2009.

                                      Gotta Serve Somebody

Hebrew numerology with its 22 letters to French's 26 but add in the elided "e" (which is worth 5) because L'Empereur Napoleon only comes to 661. Then to establish his own significance, the Count translates his own name, changes its spelling, adds his nationality, elides an unwanted "e", and, sure enough, there he is – God's antidote to Napoleon's invasion of Russia!

Two more personal favourites – one recent President of the United States of America had three names that were six letters long, *Ronald Wilson Reagan!* The other is that the Internet or World Wide Web's acronym of www is in Hebrew *vav vav vav* and *vav* has the equivalent of 6. However, in Jewish thinking, these numbers should be added, making 18 rather than 666.[144]

Others, still arguing for a compulsory international currency, give up on the name and insist that the number must be every individual having a kind of bank account number consisting of three clusters of six digits (i.e. 18 digit long numbers), which would work for 999,999,999,999,999,999 people. Or for half that number, if we were each allowed two accounts…

Summary

The number 666 has excited much conjecture over the last 2,000 years:

(i) Many have tried to decode the names of particular individuals, using numeric values of Greek, Hebrew, Aramaic or Latin letters, but as Irenaeus pointed out in the 2nd Century, this works for so many as to be useless.

(ii) Some have pinned their hopes on the Sibylline Oracles legend of *Nero redivivus*, i.e. Nero coming back after he

---

144   www.jewfaq.org/alephbet.htm, 30 May, 2011. But should we trust any explanation coming from www…?!

committed suicide, and try to make his name into 666 by interchanging languages and spelling. Augustine dismissed this in the 5th Century, and so should we.

(iii) Others, including most of the 16th Century Reformers, have believed that the Antichrist is the Papacy, and therefore every successive Pope. The papal title *Vicarius Christi,* the Vicar of Christ, is literally, 'the one in the place of Christ'. As established in *Slouching Towards Bethlehem,* there have indeed been times in church history when the Popes *and* the Reformers acted under the influence of the spirit of antichrist but there is no literal connection with 666.

(iv) In the 1970s, it was popularly held that the papal crown was inscribed with *Vicarius Filii Dei,* literally, 'in the place of the Son of God', which adds up to 666 if you use only the relevant Roman numerals. However, there is no such crown and the title seems to have originated in Andreas Helwig's brain-storming in 1612.

(v) Some think the number should be 616 but, as Irenaeus testified, it should not.

(vi) Others argue from its Greek appearance, *chi xi stigma,* where *chi* = 600, *xi* = 60 and *stigma* = 6, that perhaps John was shown Arabic words and an Islamic symbol which he faithfully transcribed but subsequent scribes wrote out as Greek letters. Those holding this view correctly identify Islam as inspired by the spirit of antichrist but the mark from incorrect exegesis.

(vii) Still others, as Tolstoy illustrates in *War and Peace,* take needlessly fanciful approaches to finger Napoleon, Hitler, Ronald Reagan and Barack Obama.

(viii) The Internet's 'www' has been suggested because in Hebrew, that is *vav vav vav* and *vav* has the equivalent of 6. However, that would also mean the numbers are added (just as the Roman numerals iii represent 3 rather than iii), making 18 rather than 666.

(ix) Also popular is the idea that 666 means three clusters of six digits which could be modern day identification numbers or bank accounts.

(x) None of these interpretations is satisfactory.

10

'Here is Wisdom...'
Anyone Can Do It

> Here is wisdom. Let him who has understanding calculate...
> (Rev 13:18)

The *NIV* translates this as, 'This calls for wisdom'. Happily, God promises all of us that...:

> if any of you lacks wisdom, let him ask of God, who gives to all men generously and without reproach, and it will be given to him (Jas 1:5)

If you are feeling bewildered, pray now – it is important that each of us finds the truth about this number for ourselves. However, it cannot be too hard because John explicitly states it can be found by anyone 'who has understanding' (v. 18), or in Jesus' words, 'who has ears to hear' (Matt 11:15).

Let us consider the text again.

The mark is specifically described as 'either the name of the beast or the number of his name' (v. 17). This means the mark can never give anyone their own identity or number, as required for the suggested international banking system. They are not being provided with proof of their *own* name or number but inscribed with the beast's – it is 'the name of *the beast* or the number of *his* name'.

Imagine, for example, the beast's name is John W. Smith and his name is translated into Greek, Hebrew or Latin, and each letter is ascribed the appropriate number in that language. Imagine that it adds up to exactly six hundred and sixty-six. What then happens when everyone is literally marked on their forehead or right hand with 'either the name of the beast or the number of his name'? They would all end up with either 'John

Gotta Serve Somebody

W. Smith' or '666' as their distinguishing feature! How would that help any merchant or bank teller to debit our accounts?

We have to stop our old habit of looking at this text through the eyes of 21st Century Gentiles. The first question we should again be asking is not what it means to us but what it meant to 1st Century Jewish believers and their associates. Only then can we safely seek to apply it to our situation.

The 1st Century Jewish church would have immediately compared John's new revelation to the inspired Scriptures they already possessed in which one book of the Law of Moses was devoted to *numbering their Jewish ancestors according to their tribal names.*

The Book of Numbers

We have already established that the marks, whether of God or of the beast, were to designate ownership. Let us now establish from the Book of Numbers why it does not matter if the mark is 'either the name of the beast or the number of his name'. Or in other words, why *either* of these is sufficient designation.

As we saw earlier, as soon as Israel came out of Egypt, God gave them marks on their foreheads and hands but then He *numbered* them. One year after the Exodus, He said to Moses:

> Take a census of all the congregation of the sons of Israel, by their families, by their fathers' households, according to the number of names, every male, head by head from twenty years old and upward, whoever is able to go out to war in Israel, you and Aaron shall number them by their armies (Num 1:2)

Did God not know how many there were? This census was not for His sake but theirs, to register all the eligible men for their armies.

Reading on, we see that it was also to indisputably locate every individual within a family and within a tribe, 'by ancestry in their families' (v. 18) as a 'genealogical registration' (v. 20).

Each one was 'numbered' as belonging to Reuben (vv. 20-21), Simeon (vv. 22-23), Gad (vv. 24-25), Judah (vv. 26-27), Issachar (vv. 28-29), Zebulun (v. 30-31), Ephraim (vv. 32-33), Manasseh (vv. 34-35), Benjamin (vv. 36-37), Dan (vv. 38-39), Asher (vv. 40-41) and Naphtali (vv. 42-43).[145]

Having been registered, they were then described as 'numbered men' (vv. 21, 23, 25, 27, 29, 31, 33, 35, 37, 39, 41, 43), counted as *belonging to the name* of the forefather of their tribe. The keeping of this name, or genealogy, was essential to the Jewish people for one-and-a-half thousand years, until Messiah came, because He had to come from the tribe of Judah (Gen 49:10, Mic 5:2, Rev 5:5). Paul therefore described himself as belonging to Benjamin (Rom 11:1, Phil 3:5), but added that this distinction was no longer necessary:

> But avoid foolish controversies and genealogies and strife and disputes about the Law, for they are unprofitable and worthless (Titus 3:9)

We see then that the men of ancient Israel were always *numbered with their father's name*. This is why the mark of the beast can be either 'the name of the beast or the number of his name'. Either way, it means the same – to bear his name or the number of his name is to belong to him.

Another reason for the numbering by tribal name was to determine which portion of the Promised Land would be their family inheritance. We have a similar situation in New Zealand today as Maori families, mine included, have been called to register their tribal affiliations in order to participate in settlements of the Treaty of Waitangi. Those who do not register will not be 'numbered' with the name for their ancestral inheritance but those who do so will be recognised under law as appropriately identified and authenticated.

This concept is also seen in the New Testament in regard

---

145 The priestly tribe of Levi was 'numbered' separately (Num 1:49, 3:6-51)

                                Gotta Serve Somebody

to Judas Iscariot. His betrayal of Jesus was particularly bad because he was one of a few highly trusted intimates, the twelve apostles, so Luke describes him as:

> belonging to the number of the Twelve (Luke 22:3)

He belonged 'to the number'. Again, when Peter describes Judas as needing to be replaced:

> "For he was counted among [Gk *katarithmeō*, lit. numbered with] us and received his share in this ministry" (Acts 1:17)

Accordingly, when Matthias is chosen to replace Judas, he is not given his own individual number or bank account but he is 'added to [or, numbered with] the eleven apostles' (Acts 1:26).

This concept of numbering is also there in Jesus' famous encouragement that, to God, "the very hairs of your heads are all numbered" (Matt 10:30). He obviously does not mean that each individual hair has been issued its own number. He means our Father knows everything about us.

And, of course, we still use 'numbered' in English today to mean 'included' or 'regarded as among, in or with' a company of people or items.[146]

None of these numbers require any kind of literal mark.

'His Number is 666'

> Here is wisdom. Let him who has understanding calculate the number of the beast, for the number is that of a man; and his number is six hundred and sixty-six. (Rev 13:18)

Here is also confusion today because we usually assume 'the number of his name' from v. 17 and 'the number of the beast' from v. 18 to be the same. This is a reasonable assumption but flawed.

As we have just seen from the Book of Numbers, the

---

146 *Concise Oxford Dictionary*, Oxford; University Press, 1985, p. 695.

expression 'according to the number of names' did *not* mean each name has a calculated value – it simply means they were counted. Nor did it mean the Israeli soldiers were issued a literal, unique service number as they are today – only the tribal totals mattered.

This is the meaning of 'the number of his name' in v. 17 – it is to show who is 'counted' or 'numbered' as belonging to the beast.

However, 'the number of the beast' in v. 18 *is* to be 'calculated'.

How are we to do that? As we have seen, if this number is a riddle to be solved and yet it is so flexible that we can take almost any name or title and make it add up to 666, it is of no value to anyone.

'Calculate…'

Firstly, we need to understand that in the Bible, 'calculating' is usually not, as we usually assume, in the mathematical sense. 'Calculating', 'marking off', 'weighing' and 'measuring' were Hebrew expressions for *comprehending* or *understanding*:

> Who has *measured* the waters in the hollow of His hand,
> And *marked off* the heavens by the span,
> And *calculated* the dust of the earth by the measure,
> And *weighed* the mountains in a balance,
> And the hills in a pair of scales?
> Who has directed [lit. regulated, measured, estimated] the Spirit of the LORD,
> Or as His counsellor has informed Him?
> (Isa 40:12-13, emphasis added)

Isaiah is not being mathematical or logistical but poetic – he is asking who among us can fully comprehend or understand Creation and the mind and purposes of the Creator to ever presume to advise Him.

Jesus likewise connects comprehending and measuring but

we often read right over it from familiarity:

We will be judged by our own standard of judgement so we
will have no excuse.

Or consider the famous writing on the wall in Belshazzar's
Babylon. It meant that Belshazzar was "weighed on the
scales and found deficient" (Dan 5:27). God was not literally
weighing Belshazzar but perfectly understanding him and thus
could perfectly judge him. This metaphor is still used today in
our courtrooms when we speak of Lady Justice holding scales
in one hand and a sword in the other. In daily life, we speak
of weighing up what to do.

When Paul prayed that all the saints would 'be able to
comprehend what is the breadth and length and height and
depth' of the love of Christ (Eph 3:19), he was not intending
us to take these dimensions literally but instead that each of
us would grasp the true, essential nature of His love.

Likewise John, when earlier in his visions he had been
given a measuring rod to 'measure the temple of God, and
the altar, and those who worship in it' (Rev 11:1). The temple
in Jerusalem had been completely destroyed in 70 A.D., so it
had been gone for almost thirty years. No results of his efforts
were recorded because it was not to be done literally. Instead,
he and all the saints were now to use *a new way and standard
of measuring* to comprehend the true, essential nature of the
temple. The old temple of stones had been superseded by the
'spiritual house', built up of 'the living stones' of all the saints
(1 Pet 2:4-5). See chapter 14, *Building a City.*

In the same way, to 'calculate the number of the beast' is
actually to truly comprehend it.

We still use this expression today – to have someone's

number is to 'understand his motives'[147] while a similar expression, to 'take someone's measure', is to 'gauge his character, abilities etc'.[148]

We also speak of trying to 'figure someone out', meaning to understand them, or to 'put two and two together'. This is not to describe a mathematical equation but the process of understanding.

Accordingly, when John wrote, 'Let him who has understanding calculate the number of the beast', he was urging us all to identify and understand *any and every* image of the beast that comes along.

Not 'A Riddle' But The Answer

We have also assumed that John was setting us a riddle for us to solve. Eugene Peterson's *The Message*, for example, has v. 18 as:

> Solve a riddle. Put your heads together and figure out the meaning of the number of the Beast. It's a human number: six hundred sixty-six.

John was not. He was actually *giving us the answer*.

This will take some time to explain but it is worth staying the course to understand.

Remember, we were wrongly assuming that only one particular man would issue this mark, usually some time in the future. However, as we have seen, this mark has actually been used throughout the 'forty-two months' (v. 5). i.e. the last two thousand years. This mark has long outlasted any particular man, having been imposed by many of the ancient Caesars in John's time as well as by Stalin, Hitler, Hirohito, Mao Zedong et al in our time.

We have had it all around the wrong way. We are not supposed to find a particular man and then see if his name

---

147 *Concise Oxford Dictionary*, Oxford University Press, 1985, p. 695.
148 Ibid.

adds up to a number. Instead, we are to *start with the number* which is itself *a revelation of the beast* and then see how and when it fits anyone.

So what does the number itself reveal, or rather, what did it reveal to 1st Century Jewish believers and their Gentile brethren in the Middle East? We have to search their source material, the Old Testament Scriptures.

There are only three other references to 666 in the Scriptures. One is a census of the sons of Adonikam (Ezra 2:13) while the other two refer to the number of talents of gold Solomon received as a tribute in one year (1 Kin 10:14, 2 Chron 9:13). I have heard a Messianic Jewish teacher say the latter two were relevant to the antichrist's number as a type but he did not establish its antitype. I could be wrong but these three references seem to be merely recorded totals.

There is, however, a major allusion to this number in the Book of Daniel.

Shadrach, Meshach and Abed-nego

Some six hundred years earlier, in Babylon, three young Jewish men had faced a terrifying ordeal:

> 1. Nebuchadnezzar the king made an image of gold, the height of which was sixty cubits and its width six cubits; he set it up on the plain of Dura in the province of Babylon…
>
> 4. Then the herald loudly proclaimed: "To you the command is given, O peoples, nations and men of every language,
> 5. that at the moment you hear the sound of… all kinds of music, you are to fall down and worship the golden image that Nebuchadnezzar the king has set up.
> 6. But whoever does not fall down and worship shall immediately be cast into the midst of a furnace of blazing fire." (Dan 3:1-6)

Most of us know this story of how Shadrach, Meshach and

Abed-Nego refused to worship this idol, were thrown in the fiery furnace and miraculously delivered, but have we noticed the dimensions of this golden image in v. 1?

They are easily overlooked today when translated into our equivalent measurements: 'ninety feet high and nine feet wide' (e.g. *NIV, NEB, Living Bible*). However, in the Aramaic original and as above in the *NASB*, the image was *sixty* cubits high and *six* cubits wide.

We cannot be exact in dating this event but we know that Nebuchadnezzar ruled Babylon from 605 B.C. to 562 B.C. and he appointed Shadrach, Meshach and Abed-Nego as administrators sometime after 602 B.C. (Dan 2:1 & 48-49). We also know that in his inscriptions:

> Nebuchadnezzar recorded his devotion to the gods… Like his predecessors, he claims to have had an image of his royal figure set up in the 'plain of Dura' as a reminder of his power and responsibilities (cf. Daniel 3:1).[149]

Daniel 3:1 confirms its location as 'the plain of Dura' but is not specific about the image being of Nebuchadnezzar. However, the Babylonian tablets are specific: these three young Jews were being commanded *to worship an image of the emperor*. They refused, with great courage and faith:

> 17. "If it be so, our God whom we serve is able to deliver us from the furnace of blazing fire; and He will deliver us out of your hand, O king.
> 18. "But even if He does not, let it be known to you, O king, that we are not going to serve your gods or worship the golden image you have set up." (Dan 3:17-18)

They were determined to trust God whether He delivered them or not. They would not worship the image of the emperor, even at the cost of their own lives.

This was the exact dilemma being faced by John's original listeners in the 1st Century Roman Empire; Revelation 13 was

---

149 *The Zondervan Pictorial Encyclopedia of the Bible*, Vol 4, p. 398.

urging them to remain faithful in the same way.

They had all seen or heard of some miraculous deliverances, such as Peter's (Acts 12:5-17), Paul's and Silas's (Acts 16:25-26) but they had also heard of the martyring of Stephen (Acts 7:54-60), James (Acts 12:2) and, presumably, Peter and Paul in Rome. As we saw earlier from the writings of Tacitus and Pliny Secundus, many more died soon after.

Daniel's inspired recording of Nebuchadnezzar's image being 60 cubits high and 6 cubits wide is not so we can calculate its area or volume but to prefigure the number of the beast because, as we will see next, the number six has its own definitive meaning.

11

'The Number of Man'
One or Any

… the number is that of a man [or, that of man] (Rev 13:18)

A complicating factor here is that the Greek is ambiguous, hence the *NASB* has, as above, 'of a man', pointing to a particular individual, but with the alternative in the margin – 'or, that of man' – as in of mankind.

Some translations have therefore gone with the former: 'the number of a man' (*KJV, ESV, NLT, Recovery Version* and J.B. Phillips); '…of a person' (*NRSV, NCV*); 'the number represents a man's name' (*NEB* and William Barclay) or '…stands for a man's name' (*TEV*); 'it is a human number – the number of a certain man' (*Amplified*).

Others, with the latter: 'it is man's number' (*NIV*); 'the number is that of man [the human race]' (Kenneth Wuest);[150] 'it is a number of mankind' (*The Power New Testament*).[151]

Still others left it ambiguous: 'it is a human number' (*RSV, The Message*).

My answer begins with the context.

Firstly, remember that Revelation 13 was to reveal to the 1st Century believers the invisible spiritual realities dominating their age. The Romans were worshipping their all-too human emperors as if they were gods because they were not listening to the Holy Spirit's revelation of Jesus of Nazareth as Messiah, God in human form; they were listening instead to the spirit

---

150   *The New Testament (An Expanded Translation)*, Grand Rapids; Eerdmans, 1961.
151   William J. Morford, *The Power New Testament (Revealing Jewish Roots)*, Lakeland, Florida, 1998.

of antichrist which was 'telling those who dwell on the earth to make an image to the beast' and to worship that.

John's revelation was therefore to urge the saints to remain firmly in the truth, despite all political, social or commercial coercion, by encouraging them to figure it out for themselves – is this Roman image really *a god or is it just a man?*

Secondly, we can be sure that any assumption of its referring to just one particular man is plainly wrong. As we have seen, this number was applicable to *every one* of the Caesars in John's day, and has been to *any worshipped emperor* ever since, including many in the last one hundred years.

Let me restate: we have had it all around the wrong way. We are not supposed to find a particular man and then see if his name adds up to a number. Instead, we are to *start with the number* which is itself *a revelation of the beast,* and then respond *whenever* it fits anyone.

Why 666?

Irenaeus added three numbers from two Old Testament accounts, Noah's flood and Nebuchadnezzar's idol. He reasoned that the Antichrist 'sums up in his own person' all the sin of 'the rebellious world' before Noah:

> And there is therefore in this beast, when he comes, a recapitulation made of all sorts of iniquity and of every deceit, in order that all apostate power, flowing into and being shut up in him, may be sent into the furnace of fire. Fittingly, therefore, shall his name possess the number six hundred and sixty-six, since he sums up in his own person all the commixture of wickedness which took place previous to the deluge, due to the apostasy of the angels. For Noah was six hundred years old when the deluge came upon the earth, sweeping away the rebellious world, for the sake of that most infamous generation which lived in the times of Noah.

He then added to that 600 the two dimensions of Nebuchadnezzar's idol that we have just considered:

> And [Antichrist] also sums up every error of devised idols since the flood, together with the slaying of the prophets and the cutting off of the just. For that image which was set up by Nebuchadnezzar had indeed a height of sixty cubits, while the breadth was six cubits; on account of which Ananias, Azarias, and Misaël, when they did not worship it, were cast into a furnace of fire, pointing out prophetically, by what happened to them, the wrath against the righteous which shall arise towards the [time of the] end. For that image, taken as a whole, was a prefiguring of this man's coming, decreeing that he should undoubtedly himself alone be worshipped by all men. Thus, then, the six hundred years of Noah, in whose time the deluge occurred because of the apostasy, and the number of the cubits of the image for which these just men were sent into the fiery furnace, do indicate the number of the name of that man in whom is concentrated the whole apostasy of six thousand years, and unrighteousness, and wickedness, and false prophecy, and deception; for which things' sake a cataclysm of fire shall also come [upon the earth].[152]

He was almost right, but not from adding these three numbers.

John actually says this number is 'that of a man' or 'of man', so how can that be?

Six is the number of the day *when man was created* (Gen 1:27-31). This defines the ultimate, definitive difference between God and man – God was, is, and always will be our uncreated Creator, and man was, is and always will be the created. Therefore, although we are made in His image, and can achieve many things, we can never be God.

The Scriptures therefore use six to emphasis our createdness, humanity and fallibility:

---

152   *Against Heresies*, Book 5, Chapter XXIX, para 2, www.ccel.org/ccel/schaff/anf01.ix.vii.xxx.html, 2 Jun, 2013.

(i)   Israel had a weekly reminder – the Sabbath. They were to work for six days but to rest on the seventh to honour the work of God as both their Creator (Exo 20:8-11) and their Redeemer from slavery in Egypt (Deut 5:15).

(ii)   They also had a Sabbath year. After six years of working the land, "you shall let it rest and lie fallow, so that the needy of your people may eat" (Exo 23:11).

(iii)   If an Israelite became so poor that he sold himself into slavery, it could only be for six years (Lev 25:35, Exo 21:2).

(iv)   Moses set apart six cities of refuge in the land of Israel, to allow for 'anyone who kills a person unintentionally' (Num 35:15). Murder was always to be punished but God allowed for genuine mistakes such as accidental manslaughter.

(v)   There were six curtains of black goat hair at the front of the tabernacle, showing man in his sinfulness being reconciled through the sacrificial system (Exo 26:9).

(vi)   Goliath, the arch-enemy of Israel in David's time, is described as being 'six cubits and a span' tall (1 Sam 17:4) while a relative had six fingers on each hand and six toes on each foot (2 Sam 22:20).

(vii)   Solomon, the wisest king of Israel, made for himself a magnificent throne of ivory, overlaid with fine gold and surrounded by twelve carved lions. It had six steps up (1 Kin 10:19-20, 2 Chron 9:18-19), reminding him every time he ascended it that he was just a man.

If only the Roman emperors had done likewise. It might have worked more effectively than the slave's whisper in a triumph.[153]

So why is the 6 repeated in 666? As we just saw, Irenaeus thought it referred to all of time:

> ... the recapitulations of that apostasy, taken in its full extent, which occurred at *the beginning, during* the intermediate periods, and which *shall* take place at the end [154]

Tom Wright agrees, seeing a reference to one of the names of God, "who is and who was and who is to come" (Rev 1:8), the unchanging nature of God's being God:

> The monster who was, is not, and is to come looks pretty certainly to be Nero.
>
> The number of perfection, not least for John, would be, we assume, 777… But for John there is little doubt. Nero, and the system he represented and embodied, was but a parody of the real thing, one short of the right number three times over.[155]

'666' could therefore very well be saying, "This is a man, was a man and will only ever be a man, so don't bother worshipping him because he is a creature and not the Creator".

There is, however, *a definitive reason* for the repetition of the sixes – it is a Hebrew poetic device. Once again, we usually overlook this in our modern translations because of our 21st Century Gentile reading glasses and incorrect assumptions that somehow New Testament thought owes more to Greek than to Hebrew origins.

---

153   A triumph was the official celebratory parade through the streets of Rome. It is widely thought that the victorious Roman general or, in later times, emperor, was accompanied in his chariot by a slave whispering, *"Memento mori!"*, i.e. remember you will die! Tertullian records the words as, "Look behind you! Remember that you are but a man!" *Apologeticus*, Chapter XXXIII.
154   www.ccel.org/ccel/schaff/anf01.ix.vii.xxxi.html, para 1, emphasis added, 2 Jun, 2013.
155   N.T. Wright, *Revelation For Everyone*, London; SPCK, 2011, p. 122.

Hebrew Rhetorical Devices

Hebrew poetry is distinctive for not using rhyme but *repetition* 'in such a way as to inculcate rhythm… Parallelism of several different kinds is very common, [including] the repetition of similar ideas (e.g. Psa 49:1)',[156] which reads:

> Hear this, all peoples;
> Give ear, all inhabitants of the world (Psa 49:1)

This repetition has at least four effects.

(i) To create a climactic impact.

Consider David's Psalm 24. The second line of each verse repeats or qualifies the idea of the first, often adding significant detail:

> 1. The earth is the LORD's, and all it contains,
> The world, and those who dwell in it.
> 2. For He has founded it upon the seas
> And established it upon the rivers.
> 3. Who may ascend into the hill of the LORD?
> And who may stand in His holy place?
> 4. He who has clean hands and a pure heart,
> Who has not lifted up his soul to falsehood
> And has not sworn deceitfully.
> 5. He shall receive a blessing from the LORD
> And righteousness from the God of his salvation.

This is today known as thematic or prophetic recapitulation and is seen every day in our courtrooms, in the closing arguments of prosecuting and defence attorneys.

(ii) To give certainty.

We use a similar figure of speech today, as when a child says, "Oh no no no! I won't do that!" which can elicit the parental response, "Oh yes yes yes you will!"

---

156 *The Zondervan Pictorial Encyclopedia*, Vol 4, p. 813.

Almost four thousand years ago, Joseph spelled this out to Pharaoh in his explanation of why the Egyptian monarch had had two dreams with similar ideas, the first featuring fourteen cows and the second, fourteen ears of grain:

> Now as for the repeating of the dream to Pharaoh twice, it means that the matter is determined by God… (Gen 41:32)

Joseph knew about dreams because of his own. In the first, his eleven brothers' sheaves bowed down to his sheaf; in the second, eleven stars bowed down to him (Gen 37:5-11). Surely interpreting for Pharaoh would have reminded him that these promises were from God and they were fulfilled soon after.

Much later, Ezekiel utters a phrase three times when predicting God's terrible judgement on Jerusalem in the Babylonian invasion:

> "A ruin, a ruin, a ruin, I will make it" (Ezek 21:27)

In Revelation, John likewise hears the heavenly voice:

> "Woe, woe, woe to those who dwell on the earth" (Rev 8:13)

The most common use of repetition in the Scriptures is actually by Jesus.

Throughout His three and a half years of teaching, Jesus gave the same messages many times as He spoke to different audiences throughout the length and breadth of Israel so the four gospels record them two or three times, often with slight variations or more details.[157] His most famous repetition, however, is so frequent[158] and familiar as to often go unrecognised as a poetic device:

> "Truly, truly, I say to you…"

"Truly" translates the Greek and Hebrew, *amen*, from the

---

157   For example, the sower and the seed in Matthew 13:3-23, Mark 4:3-20 and Luke 8:5-18.

158   John 1:51; 3:3, 5 & 11; 5:19, 24 & 25; 6:26, 32, 47 & 53; 8:34, 51 & 58; 10:1 & 7, 12:24; 13:16, 20, 21 & 38; 14:12; 16:20 & 23; 21:18.

Hebrew verb *aman*, which means to confirm or support.[159] We see then that the Lord takes the word used to confirm and repeats it, making what follows absolutely certain as well as memorable.

(iii) To express depth of feeling

You can almost feel David's grief over Absalom:

> "O my son Absalom, my son, my son Absalom!
> Would I had died instead of you, O Absalom, my son, my son!"
> (2 Sam 18:33)

When it comes to prouncements of judgement, we can all too often misread some of them as railing accusations but consider the depth of pathos in Jeremiah's prophecy:

> "O land, land, land,
> Hear the word of the LORD!" (Jeremiah 22:29)

He was known as the Weeping Prophet, rather than the Angry Prophet, for good reason (Jer 9:1, 13:17; Lam 2:11).
We should especially hear the lament of Jesus:

> 34. "O Jerusalem, Jerusalem, the city that kills the prophets and stones those sent to her! How often I wanted to gather your children together, just as a hen gathers her brood under her wings, and you would not have it!" (Luke 13:34)

In what may be the most famous words of worship, first Isaiah then John hears the heavenly seraphim and cherubim wholeheartedly crying out:

> "Holy, holy, holy is the LORD..." (Isa 6:3 and Rev 4:8)

To better appreciate this today, we may need to stop and listen to these words spoken out loud, or perhaps to Handel's magnificent *Hallelujah Chorus*.

---

159 *NAS Exhaustive Concordance of the Bible*, Nashville; Holman, 1981, p. 1490.

(iv) To demonstrate consistency.

For many years I was puzzled by Paul's explanation in 2 Cor 13:1-3 that his repeating of a statement fulfilled Deuteronomy 17:6, 'every fact is to be confirmed by the testimony of two or three witnesses'. This seemed unreasonable to me since he was only one witness and confirming his own testimony. Now, however, I see that his persisting in his message was an evidence that it was the word of God which 'abides' or 'stands forever' (Isa 40:8) or 'unwavering' (Jas 3:17). This is not as unreasonable as I used to think because in our courts today, we recognise that any change in a witness's testimony is evidence of unreliability. Paul is simply 'sticking to his story' and drawing the Corinthians' attention to it so that they will know the certainty of his words.

Repetition of Numbers

Besides ideas, words and testimonies, in Hebrew thinking numbers are also repeated for effect. The number 10 was repeated in the dimensions of the Tabernacle's Holy of Holies: 10 cubits wide by 10 cubits long by 10 cubits high. This symbolised that truly '*all* the fulness of God' dwelt in that place and thus foreshadowed the Incarnation (Col 2:9).

We also find the multiplication of numbers, much as we do in English today:

> Thousands upon thousands were attending Him,
> And myriads upon myriads [Lit. 10,000 x 10,000] were standing before Him. (Dan 7:10)

> The number of the armies of the horsemen was two hundred million [Lit. twice 10,000 x 10,000] I heard the number of them. (Rev 9:16)

There is, however, one particularly relevant example for us – Lamech's boast to his wives:

> "Adah and Zillah, listen to my voice,
> You wives of Lamech, give heed to my speech,
> For I have killed a man for wounding me;
> And a boy for striking me;
> If Cain is avenged *sevenfold*,
> Then Lamech *seventy-sevenfold*"
> (Gen 4:23-24, emphasis added)

As we saw at the beginning of this book, God had promised Cain that if anyone harmed him, He would punish them "sevenfold". This idea of being punished seven times was well-established in ancient Israel. In Leviticus 26:18-28, God made four promises to strike Israel seven times for their sins; the blood of sin offerings was required to be sprinkled seven times.[160]

It is important that we recognise this was not a literal, disproportionate response (how was God to punish anyone who killed Cain? Put them to death seven times by resurrecting them six times?) but rather a metaphorical expression meaning justly, completely or perfectly.

It originates from the seventh day or Sabbath, when God rested from all His works – He had finished Creation to the state of goodness or perfection, i.e. nothing was wrong or lacking (Gen 1:31). God's striking Israel seven times was to punish their sins perfectly, and the blood being sprinkled seven times was to make perfect atonement for them.

Notice now how Lamech constructs his boast – he takes the number God used, "sevenfold", and repeats the number to make seventy-sevenfold. Obviously, he too is not being literal but saying that if he was slighted by anyone, his vengeance would be even more certain than God's.

---

160 Leviticus 4:6 and 17; 8:11; throughout chapters 14 and 26; Numbers 19:14.

"Seventy Times Seven"?

This is the basis for Jesus' famous answer to Peter regarding forgiveness which has often been mistranslated as below:

> Then Peter came and said to Him, "Lord, how often shall my brother sin against me and I forgive him? Up to seven times?" Jesus said to him, "I do not say to you, up to seven times, but up to *seventy times seven*" (Matt 18:21-22, emphasis added)

Before we look at the mistranslation, we need to first understand why Peter asks, "Up to seven times?" Why not three, six or ten? Because he is Jewish and their seven can have the metaphorical meaning as above – he thinks that if God's punishing seven times means perfectly justly, then forgiveness might work the same way. Jesus' answer is not correcting him but affirming and doubly confirming this idea. He does that by repeating the number seven.

So why "seventy times seven"?

For many years I sought in vain for any meaning in "seventy *times* seven" from what seemed to be its only other mention in Scripture, in Daniel 7:24 where, as we saw in Book 1, Gabriel refers to "seventy *weeks*" or 490 years. However, I was finally able to establish that Matthew 18:22 was mistranslated in the *NASB* (and *KJV, RSV, NEB* and *Amplified*) and should be "seventy-seven times".[161] Many translations today have a margin note that the phrase is ambiguous so it is either seventy times seven (490) or seventy-seven, the latter being used in the *New International Version, New Revised Standard Version* and *Contemporary English Version*.

This is because the Greek, *hebdomekontakis hepta*, is literally "seventyfold seven" so some translators take it to mean 'seventy times multiplied by seven' while others, 'seventy times *plus* seven'.

---

161 Thanks to Elizabeth Rowe for her help.

                      Gotta Serve Somebody

Happily, this ambiguity can be removed, thanks to the Septuagint, the Greek translation of the Hebrew Old Testament made in the 3rd Century B.C. and often quoted by Jesus and the New Testament writers. The Septuagint has Lamech saying *hebdomekontakis hepta* in Genesis 4:24 where the Hebrew is not ambiguous but explicit: seventy *and* seven times.

We see therefore Jesus is quoting Lamech's phrase, contrasting his boast of utter vindictiveness with His own standard of perfect forgiveness. Accordingly, He reworks Peter's offer of forgiving 7 times to become 77 times.

So, Why 666 Again?

Some may wonder why tidying up this mistranslation matters because 'either way, we get the idea'.

It matters firstly because we re-discover Jesus' original, profound illustration. Is it not much better clarified than when we thought He was being vague?

Obviously, neither Lamech nor Jesus intended anyone to actually count up every actual offence or punishment. Their "seventy-seven" repeated the number seven to give emphasis and certainty to the points they were making. And it clearly works as a poetic device because we all remember it, even if we have not fully understood it.

Secondly, and this is very important, it is because of this seemingly trivial mistranslation that we have for many years overlooked this Biblical use of repeated numbers and how it applies to the number of the beast.

What then are we supposed to make of the number 6 twice repeated as in the beast's 666?

(i)   That 'every fact is to be confirmed by two *or three* witnesses' (Deut 19:15).

(ii) That it is to make *the measure of six* only more certain.

Despite any and all claims that any emperor or king is God incarnate, *the measure or nature of the beast and its image is that of mere man.* Only Jesus Christ is God incarnate and every antichrist, even when working miracles, is only human.

(iii) We are also to remember Daniel's dimensions of Nebuchadnezzar's golden image of himself as a divine emperor as being *sixty* cubits and *six* cubits. Any god-emperor, being himself a living, breathing image, adds another dimension to an inanimate image of himself so his measure is six hundred and sixty and six.

Any way we look at the image of the beast, he is only ever just a man and, while deserving honour as a legitimate authority (Rom 13:1-7, 1 Pet 2:13-17), is never due worship.

Lastly, why did Lamech and Jesus say 70 plus 7? Why not say 7 twice? And John's 600 plus 60 plus 6 – why not just say, as we do, 6 three times? Because Hebrew numbers are like Roman numerals and therefore:

> Hebrew numbers just don't work that way. In Hebrew numerals, the position of the letter/digit is irrelevant; the letters are simply added up to determine the value. To say that Vav-Vav-Vav is six hundred and sixty-six would be like saying that the Roman numeral III is one hundred and eleven. The numerical value of Vav-Vav-Vav in Hebrew would be 6+6+6=18.[162]

Summary of 'the Number of His Name'

We find then:

(i) There have been innumerable attempts, and extraordinary ingenuity displayed, to anchor the number to one man. However, as Irenaeus commented

---

162 Tracey R. Rich, *Judaism 101*, www.jewfaq.org/alephbet.htm, 31 May, 2011.

in the 2nd Century, what is the point when "many names can be found possessing the number mentioned; and the same question will, after all, remain unsolved"? Eighteen hundred years later, we have only more names.

(ii) John says that all that is needed is 'wisdom' and 'understanding'. It seems clear he expected it to be understood by any *disciple*, anyone with ears to hear. We have over-complicated it all.

(iii) 1st Century Jewish followers of Jesus, on hearing this concept of naming and numbering, would have immediately been reminded of their ancestors being numbered according to the names of their tribal forefathers, as described in the Book of Numbers. This was not strange or obscure for them – Numbers comprised one fifth of their most treasured possession, the revelation of God in the Torah or Law of Moses.

(iv) The numbers ascribed to their forefathers were not separate numbers for each individual but meant instead that each individual was numbered, counted or included as bearing or belonging to their patriarch's name which gave them their tribal identity.

(iv) 'Calculating', 'marking off', 'weighing' and 'measuring' were standard Hebraic metaphors for *comprehending*. When the metaphor was used, no one was being asked to use numbers to solve a mathematical or linguistic puzzle but to simply 'put two and two together'.

(v) The life and death issue facing many of the 1st Century disciples was that of emperor-worship. If they refused, they could be killed. John was confirming what anyone who was 'wise and understanding' would have already known – their emperor, any emperor, that they were called to worship was not, is not, and never will be

God incarnate but is merely a man: 'The number is that of man'.

(vi) They were not, and we are not, supposed to identify a particular man and then see if his name adds up to a number. Instead, we are all to *start with the number,* which identifies the nature of the image of the beast, i.e. that it is a man, and then identify the image *whenever it occurs.* Accordingly, in John's day it was every Roman emperor who claimed divine honours; in our day, it is every emperor of any nationality who has done or is doing likewise, knowingly or not.

(vii) The number six as the measure of any antichrist is first alluded to in Daniel when the emperor Nebuchadnezzar set up a golden image of himself which measured 60 cubits high and 6 cubits wide.

(viii) Writing the number as 600 plus 60 plus 6 was John's way of simply repeating the number 6, just as Lamech and Jesus did with the number 7 when they added it to 70. This was an ancient Jewish poetic device to draw attention, make memorable and confirm as certain.

(ix) Just as single Roman numerals cannot be repeated without being added, i.e. III is to be read as 3, not one hundred and eleven, John had to write 600, 60 and 6. If he had simply written the number 6 three times, the Jewish disciples would have added them to make 18.

(x) This was no mere amusement with numbers – those refusing to worship the emperor in John's day were often executed so they needed to be absolutely certain of their grounds for refusing.

12
The 144,000
Literal or Metaphorical?

We now come to consider the 144,000 in Revelation 14 who, as mentioned earlier, bear the names of God and of Messiah on their foreheads:

> 1. And I looked, and behold, the Lamb was standing on Mount Zion, and with Him one hundred and forty-four thousand, having His name and the name of His Father written on their foreheads.

John hears them singing a unique song:

> 2. And I heard a voice from heaven, like the sound of many waters and like the sound of loud thunder, and the voice which I heard was like the sound of harpists playing on their harps.
> 3. And they sang a new song before the throne and before the four living creatures and the elders; and no one could learn the song except the one hundred and forty-four thousand who had been purchased from the earth.

They also have some particular characteristics:

> 4. These are the ones who have not been defiled with women, for they have kept themselves chaste. These are the ones who follow the Lamb wherever He goes. These have been purchased from among men as first fruits to God and to the Lamb.
> 5. And no lie was found in their mouth; they are blameless.
> (Rev 14:1-5)

This is the second reference to this unique number of people because, as we saw earlier in studying the marks of God, in Revelation 7 John saw them receiving 'the seal of the living God… on their foreheads' (vv. 2-3). He adds:

> And I heard the number of those who were sealed, one hundred

> and forty-four thousand sealed from every tribe of Israel…
> (Rev 7:4)

John then goes on to name twelve tribes of Israel but with two omitted.

Possible Interpretations

There has been almost as much speculation about this company as there has been about the mark of the beast. For example, the Jehovah's Witnesses are well-known for their claim that it is being fulfilled by and among them:

> [In 1904], the first president of the Watch Tower Society, Charles T. Russell, recognized the 144,000 to be a literal number of individuals making up a spiritual Israel… In 1930, the Watch Tower Society's second president, J.F. Rutherford… stated: "The 144,000 members of the body of Christ are thus in the assembly shown as selected and anointed, or sealed".[163]

Today the Jehovah's Witnesses number over 4 million and believe that there are only 144,000 "anointed Christians" among them who will go to heaven while the rest of them will live as immortals on the earth.[164]

Amongst orthodox Christians, Dispensationalism is a widely-held view of Scripture, popularised by the Schofield Reference Bible. In this view, the 144,000 are a literal number of Jewish-only evangelists, appointed during the Great Tribulation to take over the Great Commission from the mostly Gentile church which has been 'raptured' or snatched away off the earth. Its teachers include a number of high profile Messianic Jewish teachers such as Arnold Fruchtenbaum[165] and Zola Levitt.[166] Zola explains with typical Jewish humour:

---

163 *Revelation - Its Grand Climax at Hand!*, New York, 1988, p. 118.
164 Ibid., p. 122.
165 http://ariel.org/auds.htm, 26 Aug, 2011.
166 www.levitt.com/beliefs.html, 26 Aug, 2011.

Of course! Why do you think the Lord has given us the kind of personality that we have?...God has given us that kind of personality so that we can be the world's greatest salesmen. And one day, during the Tribulation, 144,000 believing Jews are going to use those skills to convert a great host of Gentiles to Jesus. We are going to push people up against the wall and hold them by the throat until they say, 'Jesus!' Before the Tribulation is over, we are going to convert more people to Jesus than you Gentiles have done in the past 2,000 years![167]

Tim LaHaye of the *Left Behind* series agrees that the 144,000 in Revelation 7 are literally Jewish but argues that the 144,000 in Revelation 14 are Gentiles and Jews who have been converted during the literal seven years of the Tribulation.[168]

So, is Revelation 14 to be taken literally?

> 1. And I looked, and behold, the Lamb was standing on Mount Zion, and with Him one hundred and forty-four thousand, having His name and the name of His Father written on their foreheads…

> 4. These are the ones who follow the Lamb wherever He goes.…

Are we to understand that John saw a literal lamb, literally standing on the literal hill in Jerusalem with literally 144,000 men with names literally written on their foreheads? That they will literally follow the literal lamb as it walks around? Would that not be incredibly crowded and awkward? Obviously, this passage is to be read metaphorically.

Others teach the number is to be understood metaphorically by breaking it into all its factors. For example, Andrew Knowles:

> God's number is 3… The world's number is 4… Twelve

---

167   www.lamblion.com/articles/articles_revelation9.php, 26 Aug, 2011.
168   Tim LaHaye & Thomas Ice, *Charting the End Times*, Eugene, Oregon; Harvest House Publishers, 2001, p. 58. See also www.discoverrevelation.com/Rev_14.html, 27 Aug, 2011.

---

is for the the tribes of Israel (the 'first people of God'
in the Old Testament) and for the apostles of Christ
(the founders of the Christian church in the New
Testament)…
3 (God) x 4 (the world) = 12 (God's work in the world)
12 (Israel) x 12 (apostles) = 144 (God's people, old and
new).
Ten is a number of completeness or perfection – so 1,000
(10 x 10 x 10) is the ultimate full and satisfying number.
The multitude of the faithful in heaven is numbered at
144,000. That's (12 x 12) x (10 x 10 x 10) – the perfect
number for a perfect people.[169]

In other words, the 144,000 are all the people of God. Craig
Koester sees it similarly:

> The redeemed, who are pictured as a group of 144,000, are
> the whole people of God, not merely one part of it.[170]

He had earlier explained from Revelation 7:

> …this passage uses two different images for the same
> reality. The redeemed are identified as an assembly of
> 144,000 in 7:4-8 and as a "great mulitude" in 7:9-17, but
> both refer to the same group.[171]

I believe they are two different images because they are two
different groups, as can be established when we unpack the
metaphors more carefully.

So, Who Are The 144,000?

Many years ago, I asked the Lord about the 144,000 and I believe
the Holy Spirit answered me. As this is my personal testimony,
it is for everyone to judge for themselves if it is true or not.

---

169   Andrew Knowles, *The Bible Guide*, Oxford; Lion Publishing, 2001,
p. 695.
170   Craig Koester, *Revelation and the End of All Things*, Grand Rapids;
Wm. B. Eerdmans, 2001, p. 136.
171   *ibid*, p. 90. See also N.T. Wright, *Revelation for Everyone*, p. 70.

He told me to consider John's natural predicament. I understood then, and still do, that in 95-96 A.D. John was an old man, probably in his late eighties or early nineties, the last survivor of the Twelve and in exile on the island of Patmos.

What more natural question would any believer have had at that time regarding John than, "What will happen after he dies?" The Lord's answer is to remind them of how He began with 'the twelve apostles of the Lamb' and to show them He is actually multiplying the Twelve by twelve again and multiplying that by a thousand! He is not finishing the sending out with John – He is just beginning!

When the New Testament closes, we do not know how many of the multitudes of new disciples had become apostles but at least ten more are named, one of whom may have been a woman called Junia, and another two were unnamed.[172] Others had been found to be false (2 Cor 11:13, Rev 2:2). At the very minimum, therefore, the number of apostles had doubled. We are not told how many evangelists, prophets or teachers there were then but they surely multiplied.

As for the 144,000 following Him 'wherever He goes' (v. 4), when Jesus rose from the dead, He was no longer confined to one geographical location. He is our omnipresent Lord and King and therefore always with us:

19. "Go therefore and make disciples of all the nations…
20. …and behold, I am with you always, even to the end of the age." (Matt 28:18-20)

This means that the Lamb can easily lead tens of thousands of apostles in tens of thousands of different directions at any one time as He equips us to make disciples. And just as He

---

172   Not counting the Lord Himself (Heb 3:1), Matthias (Acts 1:26), Paul and Barnabas (Acts 14:4), James the Lord's brother (Gal 1:19) Silvanus (a.k.a. Silas) and Timothy (1 Thess 2:6, cf. 1:1), Apollos (1 Cor 4:6-9), Epaphroditus (Phil 2:25), Andronicus and Junias or Junia (Rom 16:7) and the two unnamed brothers (2 Cor 8:23).

sent out the Twelve to preach the gospel of His Kingdom to Israel (Matt 10:5-6), John's vision shows Him sending out tens of thousands of apostles to every nation on the earth.

As a recent example, how did China hear the gospel so dramatically after 1948? Mao Zedong came to power then, outlawing Christianity, expelling all the European apostles (those we today call 'missionaries') and persecuting about 3.3 million Catholics and 750,000 Protestants. There are now estimated to be 21 million Catholics and 84 million Protestants, almost 8% of the population![173]

How did that happen? Where did all these believers come from? From thousands, perhaps tens of thousands, of Chinese apostles going from house to house, city to city, preaching the gospel to them.

And what did John see immediately following his two visions of the 144,000?

In Revelation 7:

> 9. After these things I looked, and behold, a great multitude which no one could count, from every nation and all tribes and peoples and tongues, standing before the throne and before the Lamb, clothed in white robes, and palm branches were in their hands;
> 10. and they cry out with a loud voice, saying, "Salvation to our God who sits on the throne, and to the Lamb."
> (Rev 7:9-10)

Then in Revelation 14:

> And I saw another angel flying in midheaven, having an eternal gospel to preach to those who live on the earth, and to every nation and tribe and tongue and people. (Rev 14:6)

173　In our first study, *Dancing in the Dragon's Jaws*, p. 38, I noted the Chinese government had recently acknowledged 130 million Christians or 10% of their population. That 2008 news report has since been disputed so I now accept Paul Hattaway's more careful 2011 figure of 105 million. www.asiaharvest.org/pages/Christians%20in%20China/Provinces/=CHINA=.htm, 31 Aug, 2011.

Over the last 2,000 years, the 144,000 have been very effective apostles/missionaries and they have had angelic help to reach 'every nation and tribe and tongue and people'.[174]

The great multitude are not the same as the 144,000, as taught by Andrew Knowles, Craig Koester and Tom Wright above – they are the fruits of the ministry of the 144,000.

Their Identifying Features

We see this understanding of the 144,000 confirmed by at least seven identifying features. Since John and the entire leadership of the Early Church were either Jewish or taught by Jewish leaders, we can be sure they all knew their Jewish history so they would have recognised them easily.

Accordingly, let us try and catch up with them before we go any further.

Firstly, how would the number 144,000 have sounded to them? Wonderfully reassuring! They would have immediately recognised that despite the emperor worship, the persecution, the martyrdoms and wild animals in the Roman circuses, despite everything, God was nevertheless building exponentially on His usual foundation of twelve.

(i) The Foundation of Twelve

How would they have known that? Because, as we just saw, in their Book of Numbers, God called for every Jewish man of fighting age to be numbered according to the names of their *twelve founding fathers*, the twelve sons of the man, Israel.

Then, as followers of Jesus, they would have known what Jesus did at the beginning of His ministry, even if it took them a while to grasp the true significance of why:

> 13. And He went up on the mountain and summoned those whom He Himself wanted, and they came to Him.

---

174 For more details of 'the fullness of the nations', see *Dancing in the Dragon's Jaws*, pp. 174-175.

14. And He appointed twelve, so that they would be with Him
and that He could send them out to preach (Mark 3:13-14)

The whole Early Church referred to these particular disciples
as 'the Twelve'.[175]

Their role and work was obviously important: Jesus chose
them to 'be with Him' (v. 14) so that 'He could send them
out to preach' (v. 14). Accordingly, they were called 'apostles'
(Luke 6:13)[176] and they were to proclaim 'the kingdom of God'
(Matt 10:7, Luke 9:2).

So, how had that worked out?

On the Day of Pentecost, the number of disciples who
gathered in the upper room were 'about one hundred and
twenty' (Acts 1:15) – they had multiplied *tenfold*. Tragically,
one of the Twelve, Judas, had turned away and betrayed Jesus
but Peter reminded them that God was not surprised by this:

16. "Brethren, the Scripture had to be fulfilled, which the Holy
Spirit foretold by the mouth of David concerning Judas, who
became a guide to those who arrested Jesus.
17. "For he was counted [lit. numbered] among us and received
his share in this ministry." (Acts 1:16-17)

Peter then pointed out that this number had to be re-
established, so they chose Matthias 'and he was added to the
eleven apostles' (Acts 1:26). In other words, they knew there
had to be twelve.

Later, when John had his vision of the nation of Israel,
as we saw in Book 1, her origin is portrayed in the crown of
twelve stars (Rev 12:1). He then sees the heavenly city whose
twelve 'pearly gates' are named after 'the twelve tribes of the
sons of Israel' (Rev 21:12 & 21). As for its wall:

And the wall of the city had twelve foundation stones, and

---

175   e.g. Matthew 26:14 & 47; Mark 4:10, 10:32; Luke 8:1, 18:31; John
6:67, Acts 6:2 and 1 Corinthians 15:5.
176   Gk, *apostolos,* literally means "one who is sent", as translated in
John 13:16.

                                        Gotta Serve Somebody

on them were the twelve names of the twelve apostles of the
Lamb. (Rev 21:14)

There is no doubt the Early Church knew that God builds on a foundation of twelve.

What then would they have thought about the number 144,000?

> 1. And I looked, and behold, the Lamb was standing on Mount Zion, and with Him one hundred and forty-four thousand, having His name and the name of His Father written on their foreheads…
>
> 4. …These are the ones who follow the Lamb wherever He goes. (Rev 14:1 & 4b)

They would have remembered how Jesus began and therefore how He was continuing:

(a)   Just as He had called the Twelve to 'be with Him' (Mark 3:14), He was now calling 144,000 to be 'with Him' (v. 1), to 'follow [Him] wherever He goes' (v. 4b), i.e. 12 multiplied by 12 multiplied by *a thousand*.

(b)   He was not going to stop when the last of 'the twelve apostles of the Lamb' died – they were actually the foundations on which He was building (Rev 21:14. Also Eph 2:20).

(ii) 'Standing on Mount Zion'

Today, we can easily mistake this identifying feature as referring to a literal, geographical location, a hill in the city of Jerusalem.

To the 1st Century Jewish believers, however, this was one of their most treasured dreams coming true. Zion was just a hill until David captured it and then Zion became synonymous with his kingdom (Psa 2:6-9).[177]

---

177   See *Dancing in the Dragon's Jaws*, pp. 15-18.

John's vision is confirming that Jesus is fulfilling all the ancient prophecies of Isaiah, Ezekiel and Jeremiah of Zion's restoration *through the re-establishing of the royal house of David.*[178] This is why at the Jerusalem council, James the Lord's brother quoted Amos 9:11-12, here in capitals:

> 15. "With this the words of the Prophets agree, just as it is written,
> 16. 'AFTER THESE THINGS I will return, AND I WILL REBUILD THE TABERNACLE OF DAVID WHICH HAS FALLEN, AND I WILL REBUILD ITS RUINS, AND I WILL RESTORE IT,
> 17. SO THAT THE REST OF MANKIND MAY SEEK THE LORD, AND ALL THE GENTILES WHO ARE CALLED BY MY NAME'" (Acts 15:16-18)

To them, this restoration was on a different kind of Mount Zion, a metaphorical one:

> But you have come to Mount Zion and to the city of the living God, the heavenly Jerusalem, and to myriads of angels… and to Jesus (Heb 12:22 & 24)

This 'Mount Zion' is 'the heavenly Jerusalem' which means, as we just saw, that Jesus is no longer confined to one geographical location, as He was when He walked about the land of Israel.

The 144,000 'standing on Mount Zion' means that they are citizens of His kingdom and are therefore not confined to the earthly Jerusalem but can be anywhere on earth.

Remember, John saw them in the 1st Century, when it all started, and his vision ends with believers 'from every nation and all tribes and peoples and tongues' gathered around the throne, including those of us from the 'farthest ends of the earth' (Mark 13:27). As shown in *Dancing in the Dragon's Jaws*, the first book in this series, we seem to be very close to that time now. The time of the 144,000 is therefore not during a 3.5 or 7 year tribulation but, like most of the Book of Revelation, throughout the last two thousand years.

---

178 For example Isaiah 4:2-6, 61:1-4; Jeremiah 31:10-12, 50:4-5; Ezekiel 34:23-26, 37:24-28.

(iii) Their Song

John hears them singing a unique song:

> 2. And I heard a voice from heaven, like the sound of many waters and like the sound of loud thunder, and the voice which I heard was like the sound of harpists playing on their harps.
> 3. And they sang a new song before the throne and before the four living creatures and the elders; and no one could learn the song except the one hundred and forty-four thousand who had been purchased from the earth. (Rev 14:2-3)

As strange as this may seem to us, it was a familiar concept to 1st Century Jewish believers because of at least three ancient songs of Israel, two by Moses[179] and one by Deborah and Barak.

The whole nation had sung the first Song of Moses by the Red Sea to celebrate God's delivering them from Pharaoh's pursuing army (Exo 15:1-18)

John refers to this song in Revelation 15 where he sees those killed for not worshipping the emperor now standing on another sea, celebrating their passing through death into the presence of God:

> 2. And I saw something like a sea of glass mixed with fire, and those who had been victorious over the beast and his image and the number of his name, standing on the sea of glass, holding harps of God.
> 3. And they sang the song of Moses, the bond-servant of God, and the song of the Lamb…" (Rev 15:2-3)

God had delivered Israel through the Passover Lamb and by opening and closing the Red Sea on Pharaoh's army. In perfect symmetry, these martyrs are celebrating their salvation through the blood of Jesus and their passing through death to stand 'on the sea of glass', beyond all reach of their emperor-worshipping persecutors.

---

179 According to Jewish tradition, portions of the songs of Moses were sung every Sabbath in the Temple. http://juchre.org/articles/song.htm, 11 Nov, 2011.

The second Song of Moses were his last words to Israel (Deut 31:19-32:44)

This song contained severe warnings of what would happen to Israel if and when they fell away but it finishes with an extraordinary promise:

> "Rejoice, O nations [or, Gentiles], with His people;
> For He will avenge the blood of His servants,
> And will render vengeance on His adversaries,
> And will atone for His land and His people" (Deut 32:43)

In the same way, the martyrs that John sees on the crystal sea are also trusting in the timing of God and waiting for the Day of His justice.

The third song was the Song of Deborah and Barak (Judges 5:1-31)

This song of deliverance was to celebrate Israel's miraculous victory at the River Kishon over the cruel regime of Jabin and his general, Sisera (see also Psalm 83:9). The victory was initiated by Deborah and accomplished by Barak so they shared honours.

These three unique songs were war stories in musical form. They were, of course, not exclusive but the celebration of a shared experience and a thanksgiving for victory by all who were actually there. In the same way, the song of the 144,000 is their celebration for victories they have seen first-hand, one in which any of us can join if we too fight in the spiritual war.

(iv) They Are Virgins?

The *King James Version* (*KJV*) of the fourth identifying feature of the 144,000 gives a correct literal translation but a wholly incorrect impression:

> These are they which were not defiled with women; for they are virgins (Rev 14:4a)[180]

---

180 The *NKJV, NRSV* and *GNT* have the same.

This understanding has led to some bizarre speculation and conclusions over the centuries. Some think it confirms the idea that sexual intercourse even within marriage is defiling so God requires a celibate priesthood or ministry.[181] J.B. Phillips translates this as, 'who have *never* defiled themselves with women, for they are *celibate*' (emphasis added).

What is again demonstrated here, as if we needed any more examples, is that we have to read it as it would have been read and heard, not by 3rd and 4th Century monks and ascetics but by 1st Century Jewish believers.

Remember, we saw earlier that those numbered by names in the Book of Numbers were the *fighting men*:

> …every male, head by head from twenty years old and upward, *whoever is able to go out to war* in Israel
> (Num 1:2-3, emphasis added)

We also need to know what every 1st Century Jewish man would know, that Israel's warriors had a particular short-term holiness enjoined on them whenever they went out to war — immediately beforehand, they were to separate themselves from the legitimate sexual pleasures of marriage.

We see this in the conversation between David and Ahimelech the high priest when David sought food while on the run from Saul:

> 4. The priest answered David and said, "There is no ordinary bread on hand, but there is consecrated bread; if only the young men have kept themselves from women".

---

181 It seems that Pope Siricus was the first to officially forbid marriage for clergy in 385 A.D., despite the plain warning of 1 Tim 4:3 and 1 Tim 3:2 and 12. *The Catholic Encyclopedia* has Epiphanius of Salamis writing around that time: "Holy Church respects the dignity of the priesthood to such a point that she does not admit to the diaconate, the priesthood, or the episcopate, no nor even to the subdiaconate, anyone still living in marriage and begetting children. She accepts only him who if married gives up his wife or has lost her by death", www.newadvent.org/cathen/03481a.htm, 18 Feb, 2013.

> 5. And David answered the priest and said to him, "Surely
> women have been kept from us as previously when I set out
> and the vessels of the young men were holy, though it was an
> ordinary journey; how much more then today will their vessels
> be holy?" (1 Sam 21:4-5)

They were *set apart for battle,* just as Moses had commanded:

> 9. "When you go out as an army against your enemies, you shall
> keep yourself from every evil thing.
> 10. "If there is among you any man who is unclean because of a
> nocturnal emission, then he must go outside the camp; he may
> not reenter the camp." (Deut 23:9-10)

This is why David was unable to tempt the faithful Uriah
to sleep with his wife Bathsheba after David had made her
pregnant – Uriah was still on duty (2 Sam 11:1-13).

Many sportsmen today, especially boxers and footballers,
abstain from sex before they compete. This is not for holiness
as in ancient Israel but because of the belief that their reflexes
will be faster or to increase their aggression.[182]

A thousand years later, the apostle Paul spelled out
temporary celibacy for married couples as an aid to prayer,
provided that it was consensual and only temporary:

> 1. Now concerning the things about which you wrote, it is good
> for a man not to touch a woman.
> 2. But because of immoralities, each man is to have his own wife,
> and each woman is to have her own husband.
> 3. The husband must fulfill his duty to his wife, and likewise also
> the wife to her husband…
>
> 5. Stop depriving one another, *except by agreement for a time,* so
> that you may devote yourselves to prayer, and come together
> again so that Satan will not tempt you because of your lack of
> self-control (1 Cor 7:1-5, emphasis added)

---

182 See, for example, http://news.nationalgeographic.com/
news/2006/02/0222_060222_sex.html and www.expertboxing.com/
boxing-basics/boxing-tips/the-real-reason-why-no-sex-before-a-fight, 17
Feb, 2013.

                                    Gotta Serve Somebody

What then are we to make of Revelation 14:4a, that the 144,000 are 'virgins'?

The *KJV* is true to the Greek word John uses, *parthenos,* because according to Kittel's *Theological Dictionary of the Bible,* it means:

> "a mature young woman". According to context, the stress may be on sex, age, or status. By a process of narrowing down, the more general sense yields to the more specific one of "virgin", with a stress on freshness, or on physical or spiritual purity.[183]

However, if we were to insist on literalism, should we not also insist on the 144,000 all being non-lesbian women?

The *NASB* [184] has retained the correct sense in translating *parthenos* as metaphorical:

> These are the ones who have not been defiled with women, for they have kept themselves chaste (Rev 14:4a)

The *NIV* similarly has 'kept themselves pure' while Eugene Peterson's *The Message* has them as 'virgin-fresh before God'. Tom Wright refers to them as the Lord's 'crack troops… elite warriors':

> It is because they are elite warriors that (strictly within the bounds of the symbolism John is using) he speaks of them as 'celibate' or 'virgins'. Ancient Israel had a clear policy about going to war; if war was justified, war was also holy, and those who fought in it had to obey special rules of purity, including abstention (for the time) from sexual relations… As usual, we need to be clear about the symbol and the reality to which it points.[185]

Their purity is in stark contrast to the impurity of those seduced by Babylon the Great Harlot who makes "all the

---

183 Abridged edition, Grand Rapids; William B. Eerdmans Publishing Co, 1985, p. 786.
184 As has the *RSV, TEV* and *NEB.*
185 *Revelation for Everyone,* London; SPCK, 2011, pp. 124-125.

nations drink of the wine of the passion of her immorality"
(Rev 14:8), especially their leaders:

> …the kings of the earth committed acts of immorality, and
> those who dwell on the earth were made drunk with the wine of
> her immorality. (Rev 17:1-2)

This 'wine of the passion' is obviously metaphorical wine but
so too is 'immorality' in this context – those worshipping the
living image of the beast are spiritually immoral. We see this
also in Ezekiel's prophecy where God spoke of idolatry as
adultery and harlotry:

> "Then those of you who escape will remember Me among the
> nations to which they will be carried captive, how I have been
> hurt by their *adulterous* hearts which turned away from Me, and
> by their eyes which played the *harlot after their idols*; and they
> will loathe themselves in their own sight for the evils which they
> have committed, for all their abominations."
> (Ezek 6:9, emphasis added)

However, God does not give up. He is willing to forgive us and
He has never stopped sending out His messengers to call us
back to Himself. These are the 144,000 apostles/missionaries,
spiritual men and women, who are not permanent virgins but
spiritually battle-ready, whether married or unmarried. This is
no more than was required of all of the 1st Century apostles –
Peter was married (Matt 8:14) as were 'the rest of the apostles'
except Paul and Barnabas (1 Cor 9:5-6) – and the married are
only allowed to be celibate for an agreed time (1 Cor 7:5).

Does this mean the number is limited to only those
ordained or commissioned as apostles or missionaries? Not if
the number is metaphorical. Paul was called as an apostle, 'not
sent from men nor through the agency of man, but through
Jesus Christ and God the Father' (Gal 1:1). I believe we may
be very surprised when we finally find out who has been sent
by Jesus.

(v) 'First Fruits...'

The next identifying characteristic:

> These have been purchased from among men as first fruits to
> God and to the Lamb. (Rev 14:4c)

Again, while this may not mean much to us today in our urban, suburban and secular environments, it was deeply significant to 1st Century Jewish believers. Every Jewish child grew up in the natural rhythm of the annual agricultural festivals, two of which were 'first fruits' celebrations.

The first ritual of First Fruits was *on the third day* after the Passover (Lev 23:5-11). It involved the priest lifting up before the Lord a sheaf of barley, the first cereal to ripen in Israel, and therefore prefigured the resurrection of Messiah:[186]

> But now Christ has been raised from the dead, the first fruits of
> those who are asleep [in the grave] (1 Cor 15:20)

Its name also celebrated the certainty that *the rest of the fruit* of the harvest was not far behind. To Jewish believers in the 1st Century, Jesus being raised from the dead on the third day provided wonderful proof that one day God will raise all of us from the dead.

This initial first fruits ritual was celebrated in the first month of their agricultural year, which is equivalent to about mid-April in our Gregorian calendar, i.e. the second month of spring in the Northern Hemisphere. Then in their third month, Israel had another first fruits ritual, the 'Feast of the Harvest of the first fruits' (Exo 23:16). Celebrated on the fiftieth day after the first ritual (Lev 23:15-16), it was also called Pentecost (from the Greek, *pentekostos,* which means fiftieth) and the Feast of Weeks (Exo 34:22), because they were

---

186 The ritual also prefigured the resurrection of 'a handful' of others (Matt 27:52-53). See the author's *The Red Heifer's Ashes (Mysteries of Ancient Israel)*, Auckland; Emmaus Road Publishing, 2001, pp. 39-42.

to count off seven Sabbaths from the first ritual.[187] Its grain offering of two loaves of bread came from the now-ripened wheat harvest (Lev 23:17-20).

Both first fruits rituals heralded the ultimate ingathering of the whole harvest in their seventh month, which included figs, grapes, pomegranates, dates and olives:

> You shall observe [in the third month] the Feast of the Harvest of the first fruits of your labors from what you sow in the field; also the Feast of the Ingathering at the end of the year [in the seventh month] when you gather in the fruit of your labors from the field. (Ex 23:16. comments inserted)

The 144,000 being 'first fruits' therefore signified the harvest of the whole world was about to start in earnest. This is how the 1st Century believers would have understood the outcome John saw in Revelation 7:

> After these things I looked, and behold, a great multitude which no one could count, from every nation and all tribes and peoples and tongues. (Rev 7:9)

And again, after the 144,000 in Revelation 14:

> 14. Then I looked, and behold, a white cloud, and sitting on the cloud was one like a son of man, having a golden crown on His head and a sharp sickle in His hand.
> 15. And another angel came out of the temple, crying out with a loud voice to Him who sat on the cloud, "Put in your sickle and reap, for the hour to reap has come, because the harvest of the earth is ripe."

This harvesting of the earth and the consequent winnowing and threshing is perhaps the most common metaphor of Judgement Day in the Scriptures,[188] being a major feature of

---

187   Paul therefore says we have received the 'first fruits of the Spirit', first poured out on the Day of Pentecost, as evidence our bodies will be resurrected (Rom 8:23).

188   For example, Psalm 1:4-5, Proverbs 20:26, Isaiah 27:12, Jeremiah 51:33, Daniel 2:35, Hosea 13:3, Micah 4:12.

John the Baptist's message and Jesus' parables.[189]

Lastly, the entire 1st Century church was called first fruits by James the Lord's brother:

> In the exercise of His will He brought us forth by the word of truth, so that we would be a kind of first fruits among His creatures (Jam 1:18)

Later in this letter, he completed the metaphor of the harvest:

> 7. Therefore be patient, brethren, until the coming of the Lord. The farmer waits for the precious produce of the soil, being patient about it, until it gets the early and late rains.
> 8. You too be patient; strengthen your hearts, for the coming of the Lord is near. (Jam 5:7-8)

It is my belief, explained in *Dancing in the Dragon's Jaws*, that a metaphorical 'late' or latter rain[190] of the Spirit is beginning to fall on the land of Israel today. If so, the Lord's coming is near.

(vi) 'No Lie...'

The next characteristic may seem at first glance to not be particularly distinctive:

> And no lie was found in their mouth; they are blameless (Rev 14:5)

After all, this should be said of every Christian (Eph 4:24-25). However, it is also a particular requirement of every minister of the gospel that they not be 'double-tongued' (1 Tim 3:8) and 'not malicious gossips' (1 Tim 3:11). They need to 'obtain for themselves a high standing and great confidence in the faith that is in Christ Jesus' (1 Tim 3:13) or, in other words, genuine

---

189   For example, Matthew 3:12, 13:24-30, John 4:35-36.
190   Israel has a summer of some four months without rainfall (June to September), relieved by the "early rain" in October and November which precedes four months of wet winter. This is capped by the "latter rain" in April and May which combines with warmer temperatures to significantly increase the yields. *The Zondervan Pictorial Encyclopedia of the Bible*, Vol 5, pp. 27-28.

credibility so that listeners can safely trust their message.

Accordingly, this is particularly required of the 144,000 who have been sent out to preach the gospel.

(vii) Numbered, Sealed and Named

With the seventh, we come to the most obvious but also most difficult identifying feature of these 144,000 apostles. In Revelation 7, they are described as coming from 'every tribe of Israel':

> 4. And I heard the number of those who were sealed, one hundred and forty-four thousand sealed from every tribe of Israel:
> 5. from the tribe of Judah, twelve thousand were sealed, from the tribe of Reuben twelve thousand, from the tribe of Gad twelve thousand,
> 6. from the tribe of Asher twelve thousand, from the tribe of Naphtali twelve thousand, from the tribe of Manasseh twelve thousand,
> 7. from the tribe of Simeon twelve thousand, from the tribe of Levi twelve thousand, from the tribe of Issachar twelve thousand,
> 8. from the tribe of Zebulun twelve thousand, from the tribe of Joseph twelve thousand, from the tribe of Benjamin, twelve thousand were sealed.

There is therefore a strong case for accepting the 144,000 as literal, Jewish-only believers. It would require at least 12,000 male individuals from each of these tribes to become followers of Jesus and accept the call to this unique work. Each of them would also need to be told by God to which tribe they belonged because most of Israel's genealogical records were destroyed with the Temple in 70 A.D. so most Jews today have no attested tribal genealogy or identity, but God is God, so it is theoretically possible.

I believe, however, the case for a metaphorical interpretation is much stronger and, in the context of the Book of Revelation, more consistent. Moreover, to understand the metaphor, all that is required today is a bit more Jewish history, history which would have been well-known by John's 1st Century listeners. It matters, for example, that although these tribes are named after the twelve sons of Jacob, or Israel as he became known, two are actually missing.

Before we look at the tribes, let us summarise the identifying features of the 144,000.

Summary of Identifying Features

The 144,000 can be understood as a literal or metaphorical number of literal or metaphorical Israelites:

(i)   Jehovah's Witnesses think it is the literal number of their adherents, whom they consider to be spiritual Israel.

(ii) Some, such as Dispensationalists, believe it is a literal number of literal Jewish evangelists who will appear some time soon.

(iii) Others believe the metaphorical number means all the people of God throughout the ages.

(iv) This study argues that it is a metaphorical number of apostles/missionaries who have been evangelising the world since the 1st Century. The Lord was never going to stop when the last of 'the twelve apostles of the Lamb' died – they were actually the foundations on which He was building (Rev 21:14).

Their identifying characteristics include:

(i)   The similarity of their calling to the calling of the original twelve apostles of the Lamb who were to be with Him so that He could send them out (Mark 3:14). John sees the Lord calling 144,000 to be with Him on Mt Zion (Rev 14:1) and to follow Him wherever

He goes (v. 4b) as the omnipresent discipler of all the nations, i.e. 12 multiplied by 12 multiplied by a thousand.

(ii)   Their standing with Jesus on Mt Zion reveals they are re-establishing the house of David, as James saw when he finally accepted that Gentiles can be in the Kingdom without becoming Jews (Acts 15:16-18).

(iii) Their unique song echoes the battle-songs of Israel, sung by the participants. This is particularly relevant in the light of the next characteristic.

(iv)   They are not literally virgins but have instead kept themselves chaste just as Israel's ancient soldiers did before battle. This was a temporary abstinence rather than a permanent state for married soldiers and therefore signifies spiritual battle-preparedness in married apostles.

(v)   They are 'first fruits' of the great harvest of the whole earth.

(vi)   Their truthfulness ensures their credibility to the hearers, a particular requirement for ministers of the gospel (1 Tim 3).

(vii) Being numbered according to the name of a tribe was also a requirement of ancient Israel's soldiers, hence for the frontline of the Kingdom of God throughout the last 2,000 years.

13

Missing in Action
Dan & Ephraim

As John listens, he hears that the tribe of Dan is not included but the number of tribes has been restored to twelve by the inclusion of the half-tribe of Manasseh (v. 6). We may easily miss this today but for any 1st Century Jew, this would have never gone unnoticed.

The inclusion of Manasseh would not itself have been considered strange because, although there were always considered to be twelve tribes, at various times they were counted differently. When Israel first entered the land, the sons of Levi became the priestly tribe so they were to earn their living from the Temple and needed 'no portion or inheritance' of the land (Deut 10:9). However, Joseph received a double portion (Gen 48:22), one each to his two sons, Ephraim and Manasseh (Gen 48:8-21), so the land was still apportioned twelve ways and Ephraim and Manasseh were often referred to as 'half-tribes' (e.g. Num 34:13-15).

In John's list, Joseph being included as a tribe (v. 8) therefore encompasses Ephraim and Manasseh, but Dan's omission requires one to be differentiated again.

Why Dan?

Why has Dan been replaced? For the same reason that Judas Iscariot was replaced by Matthias.

In all wars, there are appalling casualties and nowhere is that more evident than in spiritual warfare where there are the very different outcomes for each of the fallen: all who are killed for their faith in Jesus enter His presence as martyrs (Rev 7:13-17);

those who seek to save their own lives by avoiding Jesus, worshipping the beast and receiving his mark will, tragically, lose their lives eternally (Rev 14:9-12, Matt 16:25).

In all wars, there can also be very different outcomes for those who go missing in action. When the war is at last over, some may return to their families from prisoners of war camps, to great celebration and honour; others may be found to have perished and be mourned; others may be found to have been collaborating with the enemy.

In spiritual warfare throughout the ages, surely the most tragic of casualties are those who have been the Lord's, even as leaders of His people, but then turned away and betrayed Him. Consider Judas Iscariot – from being counted one of the Twelve, potentially one of the most significant men in all of human history whose name could have been eternally on one of the foundation stones of New Jerusalem, his name is today a by-word for treachery. His place had to be taken by Matthias (Acts 1:26).

In the same way, Dan's place has been taken here by Manasseh.

The tribe of Dan became a type, a metaphor, for those disgracing themselves, for those who have left 'the holy nation' by their own choices and often at great cost to others. We see this in Jacob's prophecy:

> Dan shall be a serpent in the way,
> A horned snake in the path,
> That bites the horse's heels,
> So that his rider falls backward (Gen 49:17)

Five hundred years later, during the time of Deborah, the tribe of Dan refused to *fight* alongside all the other tribes (Jud 5:17 cf. 5:23) despite being the second strongest tribe after Judah (Num 1:39, 26:42-43). Soon after, they captured Laish, the northernmost city in what became the land of Israel, renamed it Dan and, despite the Tabernacle being in Shiloh, set up

Gotta Serve Somebody

their own shrine for worship of a graven image (Jud 18:30-31).

Five hundred years later again, Dan hosted one of the two shrines to the golden calves which, just as Jacob predicted, caused many in Israel to stumble (1 Kin 12:29-30).

Why Ephraim?

What then of the tribe of Ephraim? Why is Manasseh preferred in this list?

After the ten tribes split from following the house of David, they formed the northern kingdom called Israel but sometimes Ephraim[191] after its leading tribe. Those remaining with David's dynasty became the southern kingdom, called Judah after its leading tribe (Ezek 37:16-19).

To consolidate his position as the new king of Israel/ Ephraim, Jeroboam set up his alternative worship system in Dan at the northern-most border and in Bethel, at the southern-most border of the land of Ephraim (1 Kin 12:26-33). Although Ephraim was rightly supposed to bear the name of Israel (Gen 48:16-20), the tribe's leading in this idolatry brought dishonour to it:

> "In the house of Israel I have seen a horrible thing; Ephraim's harlotry is there, Israel has defiled itself" (Hos 6:10)

We also see in the 'dark sayings of old' in Psalm 78 that Ephraim is used as a type of 'a stubborn and rebellious generation' when all following generations were warned to...:

> 8. ...not be like their fathers,
> A stubborn and rebellious generation,
> A generation that did not prepare its heart
> And whose spirit was not faithful to God.
> 9. The sons of Ephraim were archers equipped with bows,
> Yet they turned back in the day of battle.
> 10. They did not keep the covenant of God

---

191   e.g. Hosea 5:3.

And refused to walk in His law;
11. They forgot His deeds
And His miracles that He had shown them.

The *NASB Study Bible* comments on v. 9:

> Neither the tribe of Ephraim nor the northern kingdom
> had a reputation for cowardice or ineffectiveness in battle
> (see e.g. Deut 33:17). This verse is best understood as a
> metaphor for Israel's betrayal of God's covenant (see v. 10),
> related to the figure of the "treacherous bow" (v. 57)[192]

Accordingly, in this typological list of the spiritual warrior-apostles of the Lamb, the names of Dan and Ephraim are left out. This in turn signifies those Christian leaders, Jewish or Gentile, who, like Judas, have had their names removed from the Lamb's 'book of life' (Rev 3:5).

Disowned

Some teach today that this cannot happen, that Jesus taught that no believer can ever be lost. They often base this idea on:

> "My sheep hear My voice, and I know them, and they follow Me;
> and I give eternal life to them, and they will never perish; and no
> one will snatch them out of My hand" (John 10:27-28)

Of course, any who 'follow' the Lord will never be lost but what of those who later choose to not follow Him? Just as the mark and name of the beast can be removed from anyone's hand and forehead through their repenting and trusting in Jesus, the Lord's name can also be removed from anyone turning away or becoming unfaithful to Him.

As a minister, I have many times remembered the warning parable Jesus gave us in Luke 12:35-48:

---

192 Grand Rapids; Zondervan, 1999, p. 818.

　　　　　　　　　　　Gotta Serve Somebody

35. "Be dressed in readiness, and keep your lamps lit.
36. "Be like men who are waiting for their master when he returns from the wedding feast, so that they may immediately open the door to him when he comes and knocks.
37. "Blessed are those slaves whom the master will find on the alert when he comes…

40. "You too, be ready; for the Son of Man is coming at an hour that you do not expect."
41. Peter said, "Lord, are You addressing this parable to us, or to everyone else as well?"

Peter, recognising this as a general warning to all disciples, asks Him to clarify so Jesus then focuses on the role of the steward. He shows how anyone He appoints as a leader to care for His other servants can make two very different choices:

42. And the Lord said, "Who then is the faithful and sensible steward, whom his master will put in charge of his servants, to give them their rations at the proper time?
43. "Blessed is that slave whom his master finds so doing when he comes.
44. "Truly I say to you that he will put him in charge of all his possessions.
45. "But if that slave says in his heart, 'My master will be a long time in coming', and begins to beat the slaves, both men and women, and to eat and drink and get drunk;
46. the master of that slave will come on a day when he does not expect him and at an hour he does not know, and will cut him in pieces, and assign him a place with the unbelievers."

The contrast is stark: if any leader remains 'faithful and sensible', he or she will receive great reward (v. 44); if instead, any begin to abuse the other servants of God (this can be psychologically and spiritually, as well as the obvious meaning of physically), he or she will be judged 'with the unbelievers' (v. 46). Like Dan; like Judas.

In our own time, there have been a number of high-profile Christian leaders who have overtly walked away and with terrible consequences. Moses David Berg, founder of the Children of God, began as a very effective evangelist and led many to faith in Jesus[193] but died in 1994 as a false prophet, promoting promiscuity and incest.[194] Jim Jones, founder of the People's Temple in California, began with a heart for the underdog and fighting racial segregation. However, in 1978, in 'Jonestown', Guyana, he led 908 followers to their deaths, most of them drinking his poisoned Kool-Aid. Similarly, David Koresh in Waco, Texas, contributed to the deaths of 82 Branch Davidians and four law enforcement officials in 1993.

These leaders presented their followers with a new, different Jesus, different gospel and different spirit, as discussed in our previous study, *Slouching Towards Bethlehem.*

Accordingly, Paul warns us:

> If we endure, we will also reign with Him; if we deny Him, He also will deny us;
> If we are faithless, He remains faithful, for He cannot deny Himself. (2 Tim 2:12-13)

God will always be faithful but He will not hold us against our will – if we deny Him, He will deny or *disown* us. This is why names are 'erased' from 'the Lamb's book of life' (Rev 3:5, 21:27).

Of course, God is 'not wishing for any to perish but for all to come to repentance' (2 Pet 3:9). He therefore gives us vast grace: King David fell into adultery and murder but was restored (Psa 51); Peter denied the Lord three times but repented (Mark 14:72). Both leaders, however, needed to turn back to be saved, as James (Jas 5:19-20) and Paul taught (1 Cor 9:27)s.

---

193 Some of whom helped me come to faith in August, 1973.
194 His daughter, Deborah Davis Berg, tells of her amazing escape in *The Children of God: The Inside Story*, Basingstoke; Marshall Pickering, 1985.

  Gotta Serve Somebody

To finish the parable in Luke 12:35-48, we see there will also be some pain for all of us who are not fully faithful and not fully unfaithful:

<blockquote>

47. "And that slave who knew his master's will and did not get ready or act in accord with his will, will receive many lashes,
48. but the one who did not know it, and committed deeds worthy of a flogging, will receive but few. From everyone who has been given much, much will be required; and to whom they entrusted much, of him they will ask all the more."
(Luke 12:47-48)

</blockquote>

In other words, these disciples will not be lost but will, for a time, have some painful regrets. This is particularly true of teachers, as James says: 'Let not many of you become teachers, my brethren, knowing that as such we will incur a stricter judgement' (Jas 3:1).

14

Building a City
Living Stones

We saw how the 144,000 being Jewish and Gentile 'first fruits' culminates in the harvest of believers from 'every nation and all tribes and peoples and tongues' (Rev 7:9). Now let us change the metaphor as Paul did, from agriculture to construction:

> 8. Now he who plants and he who waters are one; but each will receive his own reward according to his own labor.
> 9. For we [Paul and Apollos] are God's fellow workers; you are God's field, God's building.
> 10. …like a wise master builder I laid a foundation, and another is building on it. (1 Cor 3:6-10)

What then are the 144,000 building? The heavenly city, New Jerusalem.

Consider its construction:

> And the wall of the city had twelve foundation stones, and on them were the twelve names of the twelve apostles of the Lamb (Rev 21:14)

The Twelve are the foundation stones because, after the resurrection and ascension of Jesus, the whole Early Church became 'devoted to the [twelve] apostles' teaching' (Acts 2:42). Jesus had chosen them to be with Him throughout His ministry, as Peter acknowledged when they sought to replace Judas:

> "Therefore it is necessary that of the men who have accompanied us all the time that the Lord Jesus went in and out among us – beginning with the baptism of John until the day that He was taken up from us – one of these must become a witness with us of His resurrection" (Acts 1:21-22)

The 144,000 are therefore completing what the Twelve began. Accordingly, the wall is itself a multiple of twelve:

And he measured its wall, seventy-two yards… (Rev 21:17)

However, we also see here a dilemma faced by translators. 'Seventy-two yards' is logistically accurate and it does help us comprehend its size but *it also obscures its typological meaning.* John actually says the wall is 'one hundred and forty-four cubits', as in the margin notes of the *NASB*.[195] A cubit is the length of a man's arm from elbow to fingertip, meaning it is approximately 18 inches, half a yard or half a metre.

What we actually need to know in order to understand the meaning of the metaphor is that it measures 12 x 12 rather than 12 x 6 because, as we have established, in Jewish thinking 6 and 12 have very different metaphorical meanings. As John was actually shown 12 x 12, the 1st Century church would have understood that God is not directing them to consider the humanity and fallibility of the apostles but rather His multiplying of their initial work.

John then sees how the whole city will likewise grow exponentially:

The city is laid out as a square, and its length is as great as the width; and he measured the city with the rod, fifteen hundred miles; its length and width and height are equal. (Rev 21:16)

Again, the translators' dilemma. This heavenly city, the ultimate destination of all the redeemed of the earth, is in today's measurement 'fifteen hundred miles' (*NASB, RSV, GNB*) in length, width and height. However, John's original hearers actually heard 'twelve thousand stadia' or 'furlongs'.[196]

---

195   The NIV adds that this is the thickness of the wall (and in margin notes, about 200 feet or 65 metres). John does not specify thickness or height but it is most likely both because we are also told that it is 'a great and high wall' (Rev 21:12).
196   As given in the *NIV, KJV, The Message.*

It is therefore 12,000 x 12,000 x 12,000 stadia or, symbolically, 12 x 12 x 12 x 1,000 x 1,000 x 1,000.

The Twelve did indeed go forth and multiply. From an initial congregation of 12 x 10, they multiplied throughout the length and breadth of the earth to become 12 x 12 x 1,000 apostles, to create a heavenly city that has the length, breadth *and* height of 12,000 x 12,000 x 12,000!

We also need to note that this city of God did not begin with the New Covenant – the wall has twelve gates on which are the names of 'the twelve tribes of the sons of Israel' (Rev 21:12). These echo the entrances of the Tabernacle of Moses: the screen of the Holy Place had five pillars, pointing to the five books of the Law of Moses; the veil of the Holy of Holies had four pillars, foreshadowing the four gospels.[197]

God has always justified anyone who trusts in Him (Rom 10:11-13), such as Abraham, Isaac and Jacob (Matt 8:11). Everyone who offered the Old Covenant sacrifices which prefigured the Lamb (John 8:56) thereby entered the city through the twelve gates. The writer of Hebrews is explicit:

> By faith he [Abraham] lived as an alien in the land of promise, as in a foreign land, dwelling in tents with Isaac and Jacob, fellow heirs of the same promise;
> for he was looking for the city which has foundations, whose architect and builder is God. (Heb 11:9-10)

So, Literal or Metaphorical?

Consider now the difference between a literal reading of this description of New Jerusalem and a metaphorical understanding.

Firstly, the dimensions can be literal and simply that size.

---

197   Exodus 26:31-32, 36-37; Hebrews 9:1-9, 10:19-20

                                    Gotta Serve Somebody

However, given the obvious multiples of twelve throughout, even those taking the description literally will surely see some metaphorical significance in the repetitions. I am just taking the metaphor as its primary meaning.

Secondly, if it is to be literal, we who believe are all headed to an astronomically big apartment block where those who live on the ground floor in the centre and want to go out will have to walk at least 750 miles (1,200 km) in any direction, or climb 1,500 miles (2,400 km) of stairs to the rooftop, just to get a bit of fresh air!

Of course, there may be no problem with this as there will be no claustrophobia in heaven and we will have plenty of time – I just do not think this would have seemed any more attractive to John's original hearers than it does to many of us today.

Fortunately, John is given several other descriptions of the city in Revelation 21, one of which is that it is 'made ready as a bride adorned for her husband' (v. 2). The other includes its famous 'streets of gold' (v. 21) in the middle of which runs 'a river of the water of life' surrounded by exquisite trees (vv. 1-2). If it all turns out to be literal, perhaps we will be able to ask for a room with a view of the park!

Summary of the 144,000

The 144,000 are described in Revelation chapters 7 and 14. Some today insist they are to be understood literally but that creates clear inconsistencies e.g. 'the lamb' they follow is obviously not literal, being a metaphor for Jesus and His extraordinary achievement; the 144,000 are fighting men yet 'female virgins' so this expression also has be understood as a metaphor.

Happily, we are given at least seven identifying features, features which may seem strange to us but would have been easy work for 1st Century Jewish believers or those taught by Jewish believers. These features have clear metaphorical meanings:

(i) The number twelve is foundational to both ancient Israel, because of the twelve sons of Jacob, and the 1st Century church, because of the twelve apostles.

(ii) John was the last of the Twelve so his vision of the Lord calling another 12 x 12 x 1,000 apostles to 'be with Him and so that He could send them out' was wonderfully reassuring to the persecuted church of the 1st Century.

(iii) Their standing with Jesus on Mount Zion showed He had restored the fallen house of David in the heavenly, new Jerusalem, thus fulfilling the many Old Testament prophecies, and could therefore lead each of the apostles in every direction simultaneously.

(iv) Their unique song is like the battle song of the martyrs in chapter 15. It is not arrogantly exclusive but, like Moses' and Deborah's songs, the singers have to have been there, to partake of the battles and sing first-hand of the victories. The number being metaphorical means anyone can learn the song if they go when sent by Jesus.

(v) They have kept themselves from women not because they are literally virgins or permanently celibate, any more than the original twelve apostles were. In ancient Israel, temporary celibacy was required of all warriors before battle and, in the Early Church, Paul encouraged it for 'the purpose of prayer' or spiritual warfare. It simply means the 144,000 apostles are battle-ready.

(vi) Their being 'first fruits to God' adds the metaphor of harvest, *the* harvesting of the whole world. Just as Israel's first fruits festivals celebrated the beginning of the harvest, these were to remind John's hearers that God would complete the work. Accordingly, the 'ingathering' of their spiritual harvest is 'a great multitude which no one could count, from every nation and all tribes and peoples and tongues, standing before the throne and before the Lamb' to worship.

(vii) The truthfulness of the 144,000 is a standard requirement for every Christian but particularly for every minister of the gospel, to gain and maintain their credibility.

(viii) Being numbered according to the names of the twelve tribes, like all the fighting men of Israel, affirms their identity as spiritual warriors.

(ix) Tragically, as in any war, there are casualties so the numbers have to be made up again by replacements. Of the twelve apostles, Judas was replaced by Matthias. Of the metaphorical twelve tribes of Israel, John sees Dan replaced by the half-tribe of Manasseh. Ephraim also has been subsumed within Joseph. This is because, historically, these two tribes housed ancient Israel's re-establishment of the golden calf worship after the death of Solomon.

(x) The 144,000 are not a literally limited number of celibate Jewish men but a symbolic muster of all the warriors of God, Jew and Gentile, slave and free, male and female, young and old, who down through the ages have been sent by Jesus to preach the gospel and have 'fought the good fight' (2 Tim 4:7). They have avoided the mark of the beast and will sing the songs of victory.

(xi) We who are the 'ingathering' of their harvest are also being built as 'living stones' into not only a 'spiritual house' or temple of God but also the heavenly Jerusalem. This city 'whose architect and builder is God' has dimensions of 12,000 x 12,000 x 12,000 that dramatically complete the metaphor.

15

Conclusions

I have argued for a very different interpretation of Revelation 13:15-18.

If it is correct, we should not be waiting for the Antichrist to take up the leadership of Europe, the United States or the United Nations. Nor should we expect him to make a seven year peace treaty with Israel, and we have nothing to fear from a new monetary system. We are not to look for his mark to be a brand or tattoo, visible or invisible (to be read under ultraviolet light), barcode or microchip.

Nor am I saying, as some have, that it was all fulfilled in the 1st Century.

We *are* still waiting for the Antichrist, i.e. a particular and final instance, but we have seen that Revelation 13's second beast is not a particular *man* but *the spirit of antichrist* which was already at work in John's day:

> …the spirit of the antichrist, of which you have heard that it is coming, and now it is already in the world (1 John 4:3)

And it had already manifested in many humans:

> …just as you heard that Antichrist is coming, even now many antichrists have appeared (1 John 2:18)

This means the mark of the beast has also been around since John's day. So, as the Bible, rather than tradition or populism, defines it:

(i) It is the mark of the State's ownership

The mark is that of the first beast, i.e. the feral State. First, John saw the people worshipping it and its ability to wage war:

> …and they worshiped the beast, saying, "Who is like the beast, and who is able to wage war with him?" (Rev 13:4)

Then he saw the second beast, i.e. the spirit of antichrist, was *inspiring* this worship and the making of an image of the first beast:

> And he makes the earth and those who dwell in it to worship the first beast…, telling those who dwell on the earth to make an image to the beast (Rev 13:12b & 14b)

This was, however, no inert and dumb idol – this 'image of the beast' was alive and active:

> And it was given to him to give breath to the image of the beast, so that the image of the beast would even speak and cause as many as do not worship the image of the beast to be killed (Rev 13:15)

During the whole 1st Century, the spirit of antichrist caused the Romans to worship, and to compel others to worship, a man – their current emperor. Accordingly, it manifested to varying degrees in *all of the emperors* from Augustus in Jesus' time to Domitian in John's.

Initially beginning in the eastern edge of the Empire, specifically at Pergamum's shrine of *Dea Roma et Augustus*, this worship spread throughout its length and breadth.

To identify who was loyal to the Empire and the emperor, the Romans used a *charagma,* a mark stamped on official documents that testified to the bearer's having worshipped the current emperor. John then transferred this technical term to a Jewish metaphorical setting to identify who was instead loyal to God and His kingdom. Accordingly, he contrasted it with the metaphorical marks of God which were pictured as being on the forehead and right hand.

This worship was, of course, no new thing. The spirit of antichrist had already manifested throughout the previous millennia in Egypt, Assyria, Babylonia, Medo-Persia and Greece, each of the empires which had ruled over ancient

Israel.[198] John was simply identifying the phenomenon as it affected the 1st Century Jews and Christians under the Romans.

(ii) Refusal has varying consequences

Instead of the mark meaning that 21st Century Christians will one day not be allowed 'to buy or to sell' (Rev 13:17), refusing it in John's late 1st Century A.D. led to exile, as in John's case (Rev 1:9), prison, as in Smyrna (Rev 2:10) and death, as in Pergamum (Rev 2:13). This was the era of the Colosseum and the Roman circuses which routinely featured criminals and Christians facing *damnatio ad bestias* (i.e. execution by wild animals).

The less intense times of persecution meant the Christians were 'only' shunned socially, stripped of civil rights, forbidden to trade in markets or associate with trade guilds, and put out of public office.

In the millennia since John's vision, as noted in our previous study of Revelation 13:1-15, there have been horrific consequences wherever the second beast has taken up afresh its deadly work:

> For example, in 8th Century China… some 36 million people disappeared between 753 and 764 A.D. In the 12th and 13th Century, 30 million "Persian, Arab, Hindu, Russian, Chinese and European" men, women and children were put to death for resisting the Mongol Khans whose empire was larger than Alexander the Great's. In the 14th Century, Tamerlane killed between 15 and 20 million. In 17th Century China, the Manchu emperors killed 25 million or 17% of China's population. Two centuries later, they put down the Taiping Rebellion at a cost of another 20-30 million deaths.

---

198 Neither was it geographically confined. Emperors were worshipped in ancient China and Japan as well as in the Khmer, Ghanaian and Incan empires. The temptation is indeed 'common to man' (1 Cor 10:13).

All of these emperors fulfilled Revelation 13:15.[199]

In the 20th Century, the spirit of antichrist has caused the worship of Mao Zedong in China, Hirohito in Japan, Kim Il Sung in North Korea and Pol Pot in Cambodia. Similarly, in Europe the Russians exalted and deified Stalin; the Italians, Benito Mussolini; and the Germans, Adolf Hitler.

All of these political leaders placed the mark of their ownership on all willing to accept it. Those who were unwilling were persecuted, put out of office or business, judicially executed or killed in invasions. Overall, this led to the deaths of some 269 million men, women and children *in the last one hundred years.*[200]

Tragically, until the Lord returns, there will always be more of these political leaders coming; the last one, *the* Antichrist, will be dealt with by the Lord Himself.

(iii) The mark also exists in religious movements

Just as the spirit of antichrist can inspire political leaders to become religious figures, it can inspire religious leaders to become dictatorial politicians.

As we saw in *Slouching Towards Bethlehem*, we Christians are not exempt. Church leaders as political powers were justified within both Roman Catholicism, from its beginning in the 4th Century until the mid-20th Century, and Protestantism, between the 16th and 18th Centuries. While the idea is now widely renounced in the name of secularism (or the separation of church and state), the desire to rule or dominate others always lies latent in all of our hearts. Accordingly, the spirit of antichrist will continue to tempt us all:

> 13. Let no one say when he is tempted, "I am being tempted by God"; for God cannot be tempted by evil, and He Himself does not tempt anyone.

---

199 *Slouching Towards Bethlehem*, p. 125.
200 *Ibid*, pp. 121 and 127.

14. But each one is tempted when he is carried away and
enticed by his own lust [lit. strong desire].
15. Then when lust has conceived, it gives birth to sin; and when
sin is accomplished, it brings forth death.
16. Do not be deceived, my beloved brethren. (Jas 1:13-15)

Any leader of any orthodox or unorthodox denomination, movement, cult or sect who is putting him or herself in the place of Jesus in the affections and loyalty of their followers[201] is manifesting the spirit of antichrist. Those submitting and following them are thereby accepting that particular mark of the beast.

(iv) The mark is openly welcomed in Islam

Muhammad presented himself as the apostle and ultimate prophet of God, the sole leader of an empire of the mind that transcends all geographical borders. He now has 1.6 billion followers[202] and Islam has no doctrine of separating 'church and state'. On the contrary, the Islamic ideal and frequent goal is the unification of all states into the Caliphate, a political empire led by a supreme religious leader.

From the beginning, Muhammad taught and personally practised the killing of those not willing to accept his metaphorical mark in the 7th Century A.D. While there have been many periods of peace over the last fourteen hundred years, between the 11th and 16th Centuries Muslims killed some 60-80 million Hindus in India and Afghanistan.

In the last one hundred years, Muslims have killed a million more 'infidels' in Armenia (1915), a million fellow-Muslims in Bangladesh (1971), and two million 'infidels' in Sudan between 1983 and 2011. During the 1980–88 Iran-Iraq war, Muslims killed an estimated one million fellow-Muslims for effectively worshipping the wrong image of the beast and

---

201   This is examined more closely in *Because of the Angels (Unveiling 1 Corinthians 11:2-16)*.
202   http://pewresearch.org/pubs/1872/muslim-population-projections-worldwide-fast-growth, 10 Oct, 2011.

therefore accepting the wrong mark of the beast.

It is therefore a mistake to confuse the intervening periods of peace as the norm within Islam; recurring outbreaks of war are. There will be no permanent peace in this world until the Prince of Peace comes.

And today the vast majority of Muslims are looking for the coming of the Mahdi[203], not Jesus, to rule the world.

(v) The number of the beast, 666, identifies it as human rather than divine

We have often read the two uses of 'number' in Revelation 13:17-18 as if they are the same but they are not. The mark of the beast, being 'the name of the beast or the number of his name' (v. 17), means its wearer identifies with or is *numbered as belonging to* a particular living 'image of the beast', i.e. as a Roman identifying with Caesar, a Nazi identifying with Hitler, or as a Maoist numbered or counted as a follower of Mao Zedong. The phrase is a Jewish metaphor used in the tribal identity of every Jewish warrior in the census described in the Book of Numbers; the number 'on' each man was immaterial.

The other number, 'the number of the beast' (v. 18), is specifically 666, referring to the humanity rather than divinity of these emperors, 'for the number is that of a man' (v. 18). This is to be 'calculated', i.e. figured out or comprehended, by anyone with wisdom to ensure we will not worship an emperor, whoever it was, is, or is to come.

The repeating of the number 6 is a Jewish rhetorical device to emphasise the certainty of the number 6 which represented 'man' as created on the sixth day. This repetition of a number is most clearly seen in Jesus' famous teaching on us forgiving

---

203 The Mahdi (Arabic, *al Masih,* lit. the Guided One) is believed to be a 'Lord of the Age' who will set up a world government. While Muslims acknowledge Jesus, or *Isa* in Arabic, as *a* messiah, they believe He will return as a Muslim to work alongside the Mahdi.

77 times, in contrast to Lamech being vindictive 77 times, but this repetition has until recently been concealed by our mistranslation of this as 70 times 7.

Accordingly, we are to respect and pay taxes to support our political leaders, but never to overdo it: "render to Caesar the things that are Caesar's, and to God, the things that are God's" (Matt 22:21).

(vi) What then should we look for next?

In the 21st Century, there may be more secular emperors who will arise and fulfill Revelation 13. China or Russia, for example, could revert to their authoritarian ways of the 20th Century. Or a completely new secular empire might arise from historically non-colonising but potentially vast economic areas such as Brazil in South America or the Congo in South Africa.

It seems more likely to me, however, that the next fulfilment will again be within what Churchill called an "empire of the mind"[204], i.e. within Islam. If that is the case, the only mark we will need to watch out for will not be an implanted super-microchip in our hands or foreheads but the preaching of 'another Jesus', 'another gospel' and 'another spirit', while we await the possible emergence of the Mahdi and the return of Jesus.

---

204 "The empires of the future are the empires of the mind". Speech at Harvard University, Sep 6, 1943.

Epilogue

In 1979, Bob Dylan released a dramatic new album, *Slow Train Coming*. One track, *Gotta Serve Somebody*, won him a Grammy Award and began:

> You may be an ambassador to England or France
> You may like to gamble, you might like to dance
> You may be the heavyweight champion of the world
> You may be a socialite with a long string of pearls
>
> But you're gonna have to serve somebody, yes indeed
> You're gonna have to serve somebody
> Well, it may be the devil or it may be the Lord
> But you're gonna have to serve somebody.[205]

Ex-Beatle John Lennon responded to Dylan's insistence on this choice of only two by writing and recording a parody:

> You got to serve yourself
> Ain't nobody gonna do for you
> You got to serve yourself
> Well, you may believe in devils and you may believe in Lords
> But Christ, you're gonna have to serve yourself
> And that's all there is to it.[206]

In an extended interview in 1980, Lennon explained:

> It is unfortunate when people say, 'This is the only way.' That's the only thing I've got against anybody, if they are saying, 'This is the only answer.' I don't want to hear about that. There isn't one answer to anything.[207]

In 2013, Dylan released an affectionate posthumous tribute to Lennon, *Roll On John*.[208]

---

205 www.bobdylan.com/us/songs/gotta-serve-somebody, 10 Dec, 2013.
206 Released in 2006 on a posthumous album, *Anthology*. www.metrolyrics.com/serve-yourself-lyrics-john-lennon.html, 9 Dec, 2013
207 *All We Are Saying*, article by David Sheff in *Playboy*, Jan, 1981.
208 http://www.metrolyrics.com/roll-on-john-lyrics-bob-dylan.html,

I readily understood Lennon's reaction, having myself held similar beliefs prior to encountering Jesus. I questioned the Lord's blunt assertion:

> "No one can serve two masters; for either he will hate the one and love the other, or he will be devoted to one and despise the other. You cannot serve God and wealth [lit. mammon]" (Matt 6:24)

On several occasions I had held two jobs, one full-time and one part-time, without any internal conflict so I could not see any problem at all in serving two masters. However, I realised that Jesus meant the conflict that arises when they require opposing responses from us. He gives the example of God and mammon (i.e. the personification and idolisation of wealth) – if God commands us to give to someone in need and we are unwilling because we would rather keep the money, we are really serving mammon.

Of course, this may also be seen as Lennon saw it – as serving yourself – but Jesus points out that at a deeper level, we indulge or resist our own desires according to our value system (ascribing 'worth-ship'). Many unbelievers avoid adultery because they value their marriage, or intoxication because they value their reputation.

For those following Jesus, however, our primary motivation is to be wholehearted love of God and our neighbour. This is what it means to serve Him.

The only other option is to *not* serve the Lord, even if we are good, upright and moral citizens, but that is the devil's option – if we choose his option, we *are* serving him.

•••

23 Jan, 2014

  Gotta Serve Somebody

Next in the series ...

In the last book in this series of five, we will consider the predicted end of the three evil characters of these first three studies – the dragon, the beast and the false prophet. We will see from Revelation chapters 16, 19 and 20 how they will gather all their forces for the battle of Har-Magedon and be brought to judgement.

Before then, in Book 4, we will lay some needed groundwork from Revelation chapter 11, of which N.T. Wright says:

> People find many books puzzling, but the Bible is often the most puzzling of all. People find many parts of the Bible puzzling, but Revelation is often seen as the most puzzling book of all. And people find Revelation puzzling, but the first half of chapter 11… is, for many, the most puzzling part of all. (There are some other strong contenders for this dubious distinction, but chapter 11 can hold its own).[209]

However, we have a new starting point: we have recovered several lost keys to understanding it from Chapters 12, 13 and 14, especially its time period of 'forty-two months' (Rev 11:2) and 'twelve hundred and sixty days' (Rev 11:3).

As you will see, these recovered keys can unlock some very difficult texts.

---

209 *Revelation for Everyone*, London; SPCK Publishing, 2011, p. 97.

Bibliography

Books

Barclay, William. 1957. *Letters to the Seven Churches,* London: SCM Press

1969. *The New Testament,* Volume II, London: Collins

Berg, Deborah Davis. 1985. *The Children of God: The Inside Story,* Basingstoke: Marshall Pickering

Blaiklock, E.M. 1965. *Cities of the New Testament,* London: Pickering & Inglis

\-   1977. *Commentary on the New Testament,* London: Hodder & Stoughton

Carlé, Graeme. 1998. *Because of the Angels (Unveiling 1 Corinthians 11:2-16),* Auckland: Emmaus Road Publishing

\-   2001. *The Red Heifer's Ashes (Mysteries of Ancient Israel),* Emmaus Road Publishing

\-   2011. *Dancing in the Dragon's Jaws (The Mystery of Israel's Survival),* Auckland: Emmaus Road Publishing

\-   2012. *Slouching Towards Bethlehem (The Rise of the Antichrists),* Auckland: Emmaus Road Publishing

Cook, Terry. 1996. *The Mark of the New World Order,* New Kensington, PA: Whitaker House

Daniels, Eddie. 1998. *There and Back: Robben Island,* 1964-1979, Cape Town: Mayibuye Books

Darwin, Charles. 1859. *On the Origin of Species by Means of Natural Selection, or the Preservation of Favoured Races in the Struggle for Life,* London: John Murray

DeHaan, M.R. 1998. *Studies in Revelation,* Grand Rapids: Kregel Publications

Deissman, Adolph, with Lionel R.M. Strachan. 1927. *Light from the Ancient East,* London: Hodder & Stoughton

Dikötter, Frank. 2010. *Mao's Great Famine: The History of China's Most Devastating Catastrophe, 1958-1962,* New York: Bloomsbury and Walker Press

Foster, Thomas. 1983. *Amazing Book of Revelation Explained!*

Blackburn, Vic.: Acacia Press

Gandhi, M.K. 1983. *An Autobiography (or the Story of My Experiments with Truth)*, New York: Penguin Books Ltd.

Gould, S.J. 1977. *Ontogeny and Phylogeny*, Cambridge, MA: Belknap-Harvard Press

Guy, Laurie. 2004. *Introducing Early Christianity: A Topical Survey of Its Life, Beliefs & Practices*, Downers Grove, Illinois: InterVarsity Press

\- 2009. *Making Sense of the Book of Revelation*, Oxford: Regent's Park College

Hedding, Malcolm. 2013. *Understanding Revelation (Preparing Believers for Their Coming King)*, Murfreesboro, TN: Intend Publishing

Hendriksen, William. 1986. *More than Conquerors: An Interpretation of the Book of Revelation*, Grand Rapids, MI: Baker Book House

Hunt, Dave. 1993. *How Close Are We?* Eugene, OR: Harvest House Publishers

Ice, Thomas, with Tim LaHaye. 2001. *Charting the End Times, Eugene,* OR: Harvest House Publishers,

Jacobs, Louis, 1999. *Concise Companion to the Jewish Religion*, Oxford: Oxford University Press

Jeffers, James S. 1999. *The Greco-Roman World of the New Testament Era - Exploring the Background of Early Christianity*, Downers Grove, IL: IVP Academic

Jenkins, Jerry B., with Tim LaHaye. 1999. *Are We Living in the End Times?* Wheaton, IL: Tyndale

2000. *The Indwelling: The Beast Takes Possession*, Wheaton, IL: Tyndale

Jeremiah, David. 2008. *What in the World is Going On?* Dallas: Thomas Nelson

Kirban, Salem. 1978. *Satan's Mark Exposed*, Chattanooga, TN: AMG Publishers

Klein, John, with Michael Adam Spears and Michael Christopher. 2009. *Lost in Translation (The Book of Revelation through Hebrew Eyes)*, Bend, OR: Covenant Research Institute

Knowles, Andrew. 2001. *The Bible Guide*, Oxford: Lion
    Publishing
Koester, Craig R. 2001. *Revelation and the End of All Things*,
    Grand Rapids, MI: Wm B. Eerdmans Publishing Co
LaHaye, Tim, with Jerry B. Jenkins. 1999. *Are We Living in the
    End Times?* Wheaton, IL: Tyndale
        2000. *The Indwelling: The Beast Takes Possession*, Wheaton,
    IL: Tyndale
        with Thomas Ice. 2001. *Charting the End Times*, Eugene,
    OR: Harvest House Publishers
Larkin, Clarence. 1918. *Dispensational Truth*, Glenside, PA: Rev.
    Clarence Larkin Est.
Lindsey, Hal. 1970. *The Late, Great Planet Earth*, Grand Rapids,
    MI: Zondervan
        1980. *The 1980's: Countdown to Armageddon*, Oakland, CA:
    Westgate Press Inc.
Lipscomb, William. 1990. *The Armenian Apocryphal Adam
    Literature*, Atlanta, GA: Scholars Press
Luther, Martin. 1969. *Luther's Works*, Minneapolis; Fortress Press
Missler, Chuck. 1999. *Cosmic Codes (Hidden Messages from the
    Edge of Eternity)*, Coeur d'Alene, ID: Koinonia House
Pentecost, J. Dwight. 1961. *Prophecy for Today*, Grand Rapids,
    MI: Zondervan
Perkins, Pheme. 1988. *Reading the New Testament*, Mahwah, New
    Jersey: Paulist Press.
Richardson, Joel with Walid Shoebat. 2008. *God's War on Terror
    (Islam, Prophecy and the Bible)*, Newtown, Pensylvania: Top
    Executive Media
Shoebat, Walid and Joel Richardson. 2008. *God's War on Terror
    (Islam, Prophecy and the Bible)*, Newtown, Pensylvania: Top
    Executive Media
Solzhenitsyn, Alexander. 1973. *The Gulag Archipelago 1918-1956*,
    Vol One, New York: Harper & Row
Spears, Michael Adam with John Klein and Michael Christopher.
    2009. *Lost in Translation (The Book of Revelation through
    Hebrew Eyes)*, Bend, OR: Covenant Research Institute

 Gotta Serve Somebody

Stern, David H. 1992. *Jewish New Testament Commentary*, Clarksville, MD: Jewish New Testament Publications, Inc.

Tenney, Merrill C. 1958. *Interpreting Revelation*, London: Pickering & Inglis Ltd

Walvoord, John F. 1966. *The Revelation of Jesus Christ*, Chicago: Moody Press

White, Ellen G. 1974. *The Great Controversy*, Mountain View, California: Pacific Press.

Wilcock, Michael. 1975. *The Message of Revelation*, Leicester, England: InterVarsity Press

Wright, N.T. 2011. *Revelation for Everyone*, London: SPCK

Books Online

Augustine (354-430 A.D.), De Civitate Dei, http://www.ccel.org/ccel/schaff/npnf102.toc.html

Irenaeus (125-202 A.D.), Against Heresies, www.columbia.edu/cu/augustine/arch/irenaeus/

Luther, Martin (1483-1536), Works IV, http://archive.org/details/worksofmartinlut009638mbp

Pliny Secundus (23-79 A.D.), Epistles, X. 96, www.textexcavation.com/plinytestimonium.html

Smith's Bible Dictionary, www.bible-history.com/smiths/

Suetonius (69-122 A.D.), Life of Domitian - http://penelope.uchicago.edu/Thayer/E/Roman/Texts/Suetonius/12Caesars/Domitian*.html

Tacitus, Cornelius (56-117 A.D.), Annals. www.earlychristianwritings.com/tacitus.html

Tertullian (160-220 A.D.), Apologeticus. www.tertullian.org/works/apologeticum.htm

Tolstoy, Leo (1828-1910). War and Peace. http://tolstoy.thefreelibrary.com/War-and-Peace/9-19

Qur'an, http://www.cmje.org/religious-texts/quran/

Wheatley, Phillis (1753-1784), On Being Brought from Africa to America, www.earlyamerica.com/review/winter96/wheatley.html

White, Ellen G (1827-1915): http://text.egwwritings.org/

publication.php?pubtype=Book&bookCode=WLF&pagenu
mber=19 http://text.egwwritings.org/publication.php?pubtype
=Book&bookCode=TM&lang=en&pagenumber=133
http://www.earlysda.com/books/ellen-white/little-flock.rtf

Bible Translations

Amplified Bible (Amp.), 1965. Grand Rapids, MI: Zondervan
    Bible Publishers

Authorised (AV) or *King James Version (KJV)*, 1611. Oxford:
    Oxford University Press

Contemporary English Version (CEV), 1995. New York: American
    Bible Society

English Standard Version (ESV), 2001. Wheaton, IL: Crossway

Good News Bible (GNT Bible), 1994. Minto, NSW: The Bible
    Society in Australia Inc.

New American Standard (NASB), 1970. La Habra, CA: The
    Lockman Foundation

New Century Version (NCV), 2005. Nashville, TN: Thomas
    Nelson Publishers

New English Bible with the Apocrypha (NEB), 1971. New York:
    Oxford University Press

New International Version (NIV), 1978. Grand Rapids, MI:
    Zondervan Bible Publishers

New King James Version (NKJV), 1992. Nashville, TN: Thomas
    Nelson Publishers

New Living Translation (NLT), 2007. Carol Stream, IL: Tyndale
    House Publishers

*New Oxford Annotated Bible (New Revised Standard Version with
    the Apocrypha)*, Augmented 3rd Edition, 2001. New York:
    Oxford University Press

New Revised Standard Version (NRSV), 1989. New York: American
    Bible Society

Recovery Version, 1991. Anaheim, CA: Living Stream Ministry

Revised Standard Version (RSV), 1971. New York: Collins

Schofield Reference Bible, 1909. Oxford University Press

The Kingdom New Testament (A Contemporary Translation), 2011.

N.T. Wright. New York: HarperOne Publishers

The Message, 2004. Eugene H. Peterson. Colorado Springs, CO: NavPress

The New Testament, 1969. William Barclay. London: Collins

The New Testament (An Expanded Translation), 1961. Kenneth Wuest. Grand Rapids, IL: Wm. B. Eerdmans Publishing Co

The New Testament in Modern English, 1962. J.B. Phillips. London: Harper Collins

The Power New Testament (Revealing Jewish Roots), 1998. William J. Morford. Lakeland, FL

Today's English Version (TEV), 1992. New York: American Bible Society

Zondervan (NASB) Study Bible, 1999. Grand Rapids, MI: Zondervan

Dictionaries & Encyclopaedia

Cambridge History of the Bible, 1963. Cambridge University Press

Concise Oxford Dictionary, 1985. Oxford University Press

Dictionary of Premillennial Theology, ed. Mal Couch, 1996. Grand Rapids, MI: Kregel Publications

Encarta 96, 1996. Buffalo, New York: Microsoft

Expository Dictionary of New Testament Words, W.E. Vine, 1975. London: Oliphants

NAS Exhaustive Concordance of the Bible, 1981. Nashville, TN: Holman

The New Bible Dictionary, ed. F.F. Bruce and J.I. Packer, 1962. London: IVF Press

The New Oxford Annotated Bible, Augmented Third Edition. 2001. New York: Oxford University Press

Theological Dictionary of the New Testament, Kittel & Friedrich, abridged by Geoffrey Bromley, 1990. Grand Rapids, MI: William B. Eerdmans Publishing Co

The Zondervan Pictorial Encyclopedia of the Bible, ed. Merrill C. Tenney. 1977. Grand Rapids, MI: Zondervan

Newspapers & Magazines
Playboy, Chicago, January 1981 edition
The Guardian, London
The New York Times, New York

Articles & Pamphlets
Bacchiocchi, S. *Our Adventist Church Has Struggled to Define 666.*
    ENDTIME ISSUES NEWSLETTER No. 144
Finch, G.A. 1921. *Superior Orders and War Crimes, The American
    Journal of International Law*, Vol. 15, No. 3
Gerstein, Kurt (1905-1945). www.auschwitz.dk/gerstein.htm, 10
    Oct, 2011
Helwig, Andreas. 1612. *Antichristus Romanus.* www.archive.org/
    details/antichristusromanus
Rekhavi, Hakham. *A Sign Upon Your Hand and as Frontlets
    Between Your Eyes.* www.karaite-corner.org, 29 May, 2009
Rich, Tracey R. *Judaism 101*, www.jewfaq.org/alephbet.htm, 31
    May, 2011
Sheff, David. *All We Are Saying*, Jan 1981, *Playboy*
Watchtower Society, New York. 1988. *Revelation - Its Grand
    Climax at Hand!*

Miscellaneous
Catechism of the Catholic Church, 1994, English edition

Websites Accessed
www.pbc.org/files/messages/3394/0322.html
www.ancient-hebrew.org/3_taw.html
http://lawbrain.com/wiki/%22X%22_as_a_Signature
www.bible-discernments.com/joshua/whatisachiasm.html
www.JewishEncyclopedia.com
www.jewishencyclopedia.com/view.jsp?artid=290&letter=P&sear
    ch=phylactery#1109
www.jewfaq.org/signs.htm
www.oxfordreference.com/view/10.1093/
    acref/9780192800886.001.0001/acref-9780192800886

www.karaites.org.uk/phylacteries.shtml

www.karaite-korner.org/karaite-faq.shtml

www.beingjewish.com/mitzvos/tefillin.html

www.chabad.org/generic_cdo/aid/102436/jewish/Tefillin.htm

http://downloads.bbc.co.uk/rmhttp/radio4/transcripts/2011_reith1.pdf

www.guardian.co.uk/world/2001/jun/11/mcveigh.usa1

www.roman-britain.org/people/tiberius.htm

www.jewishencyclopedia.com/articles/14346-tetragrammaton

www.hebrew4christians.com/Names_of_G-d/Adonai/adonai.html

www.jewishencyclopedia.com/articles/840-adonai

www.jewishvirtuallibrary.org/jsource/judaica/ejud_0002_0006_0_05937.html

www.textexcavation.com/plinytestimonium.html

http://untreaty.un.org/ilc/texts/instruments/english/draft%20articles/7_1_1950.pdf

www.auschwitz.dk/gerstein.htm

www.nytimes.com/2010/12/16/opinion/16iht-eddikotter16.html

www.cecc.gov/pages/virtualAcad/his/prc.php

www.bible-researcher.com/persecution.html#libelli

www.archive.org/stream/lightfromancientoodeis#page/n483/mode/2up

www.ucl.ac.uk/ceelbas/workshops/international_elites_workshops/Shkaratan_Paper_Lane_Workshop.pdf

http://penelope.uchicago.edu/~grout/encyclopaedia_romana/gladiators/nero.html

www.preteristarchive.com/BibleStudies/JewishSources/Apocalyptic/0080_sibylline-4_apocalyptic.html

www.mountainretreatorg.net/classics/necreform4.html

www.archive.org/details/antichristusromanus

www.csad.ox.ac.uk/POxy/beast616.htm

www.ccel.org/ccel/schaff/anf01.ix.vii.xxxi.html

www.csad.ox.ac.uk/POxy/beast616.htm

www.ccel.org/ccel/schaff/anf01.ix.vii.xxxi.html

www.codex-sinaiticus.net/en/manuscript.aspx?book=59&chapter

=13&lid=en&side=r&verse=18&zoomSlider=0
www.fivedoves.com/rapture/2009/Obama_Rev1318.html
www.jewfaq.org/alephbet.htm
http://ariel.org/auds.htm
www.levitt.com/beliefs.html
www.lamblion.com/articles/articles_revelation9.php
www.discoverrevelation.com/Rev_14.html
www.asiaharvest.org/pages/Christians%20in%20China/
    Provinces/=CHINA=.htm
http://juchre.org/articles/song.htm
www.newadvent.org/cathen/03481a.htm
http://news.nationalgeographic.com/
    news/2006/02/0222_060222_sex.html
www.expertboxing.com/boxing-basics/boxing-tips/the-real-
    reason-why-no-sex-before-a-fight
http://pewresearch.org/pubs/1872/muslim-population-
    projections-worldwide-fast-growth
www.bobdylan.com/us/songs/gotta-serve-somebody
www.metrolyrics.com/roll-on-john-lyrics-bob-dylan.html
www.metrolyrics.com/serve-yourself-lyrics-john-lennon.html

Gotta Serve Somebody

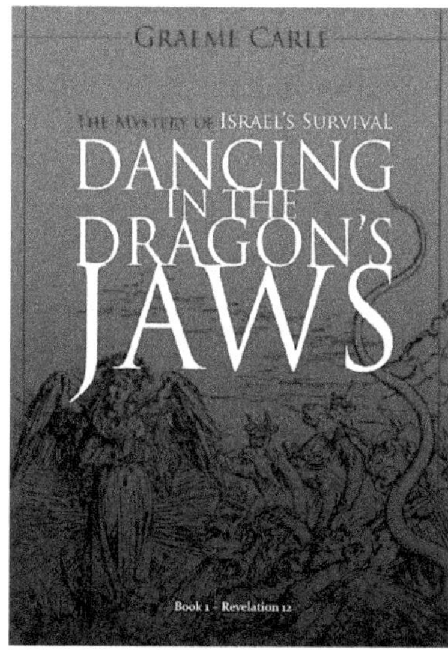

Book 1 in the series

Dancing in the Dragon's Jaws

The Mystery of Israel's Survival

Graeme Carlé

Why is the Book of Revelation so misunderstood? Wasn't its whole point to give revelation? Well, in typically Jewish manner, yes and no.

The Book of Revelation was written as an apocalypse, a Jewish literary genre which also includes the extraordinary Books of Daniel and Zechariah. Profound truths were concealed from outsiders and opponents using elaborate symbolism, to be understood only by those properly taught – as Jesus explains in Matthew 13:10-13.

The apostle John's original 1st Century audience, having been led by Jewish Christians, would have readily understood his imagery from Jewish history. His plagues echo the ten plagues of Israel's exodus; his seven trumpets resonate of the Old Testament battle for Jericho.

Many think the keys to unlocking the Book of Revelation are lost. Not so. We still have Old Testament history and, for those who know where to look, full explanations of its symbols in the New Testament. What we need is the humility to learn from the 1st Century Jewish believers the mysteries of the woman, the Messiah, the dragon, the comings of Elijah, and 'the times of the Gentiles'. From these we can understand God's continuing purpose for Israel.

Available from
Emmaus Road Publishing
PO Box 38 823 Howick, Auckland 2014 New Zealand
www.emmausroad.org.nz

ISBN 978-09582746-5-4

Book 2 in the series

Slouching Towards Bethlehem

The Rise of the Antichrists

Graeme Carlé

The Lost Keys of Revelation?

It is often thought today that the keys to understanding the Book of Revelation have been lost and are irretrievable – but they're not. They were just buried under centuries of rubble created by the Gentile church's foolish attempts to distance itself from its Jewish foundations. If, like any archaeologist, we dig carefully we can rediscover them.

In *Dancing in the Dragon's Jaws*, we found one key to understanding Revelation chapter 12 is the metaphorical "time, times and half a time" and we unlocked the last 4,000 years of Jewish history.

This book, *Slouching Towards Bethlehem*, unlocks Revelation chapter 13 and the last 2,000 years of the Christian era, with startling results. Not only can we now understand the forces shaping history and the deaths of some 270 million in 20th Century genocides but we can also project the future of Israel and the Middle East.

Available from
Emmaus Road Publishing
PO Box 38 823 Howick, Auckland 2014 New Zealand
www.emmausroad.org.nz

ISBN 978-0-9582746-8-5

Book 4 in the Revelation series

Silencing the Witnesses

Jerusalem & the Ascent of Secularism

Graeme Carlé

Moses and Elijah back from the dead?

The most popular interpretation of Revelation 11 today is *literal* – that Moses and Elijah are soon to reappear in the streets of Jerusalem as witnesses, to preach for three and a half years, then be killed by a metaphorical beast (a man called the Antichrist) before being resurrected again after three and a half days.

The most common academic view today, however, is that these are all *metaphorical* images, referring to the church being persecuted initially by the Romans, today by the whole world, but ultimately vindicated.

In this book, Graeme Carlé takes the metaphorical approach but from a Jewish perspective. The Early Church was, after all, led by Jewish disciples and/or Gentiles taught by Jewish disciples. He shows how the two witnesses would have been understood by John's 1st Century audience to be the Law and the Prophets, making essential connections with Jesus' parable of the rich man and Lazarus, and with Paul's two Jerusalems in Galatians 4.

In doing so, Graeme surveys the effects of the Law over 4,000 years of Jewish history, how it still applies to every Jew not under the New Covenant, and how it is relevant for all of us today.

Available from
Emmaus Road Publishing
PO Box 38 823 Howick, Auckland 2014 New Zealand
www.emmausroad.org.nz

ISBN 978-0-9941058-2-0

Other books by Graeme Carlé

Because of the Angels

(Unveiling 1 Corinthians 11:2-16)
This text has been largely lost to today's church because we have badly misunderstood some of Paul's Hebrew presuppositions regarding 'head', 'covering', the fall of Satan and spiritual warfare. Liberating for men and women of God as it restores much needed revelation on gender differences and relationships as well as the mystery of the Nazarite vow.

The Red Heifer's Ashes

(Mysteries of Ancient Israel)
Considered by Orthodox rabbis to be the greatest mystery of the Law of Moses, this is an astonishing revelation of Messiah. Every detail is gently unfolded as the reader today follows a supernatural path through the whole of the Old Testament, just as the two disciples did on the road to Emmaus.

Born of the Spirit

(A study guide for new believers)
This interactive Bible study is for all who want to develop their personal spirituality by checking the foundations of what Jude the Lord's youngest brother called 'the faith which was once for all delivered to the saints' (Jude 3). Avoiding all denominational allegiances, find out for yourself how God wants us to love, live and learn.

Eating Sacred Cows
A Closer Look at Tithing

Graeme Carlé

To tithe or not to tithe?

Tithing is one of the most misunderstood and abused aspects of modern day religion, and there are fine Christian leaders on both sides of the issue. Images of tele-evangelists and pastors living extravagant lifestyles can fuel resentment and mockery, but the defence is often that God's 'prosperity' ideal is being upheld (at least for the receiver of tithes).

But what of the givers?

Many Christians testify how God has blessed them for tithing, but many others are disappointed, often too ashamed to speak openly in case they are 'letting God down'. Sermons on tithing almost always quote Malachi's rebuke of ancient Israel, "You are cursed for you are robbing God! Bring the whole tithe into the storehouse…" (Malachi 3:8–9). But what exactly did Malachi mean? Doesn't God still want us to tithe? Well, not in the way we are usually taught today.

Citing Biblical texts about tithing that are rarely, if ever, referred to by those teaching tithing to fund the church, Graeme Carlé shows instead how God wants us to receive a revelation of His goodness as we take time off to enjoy annual holidays. He also wants us to be generous, giving freely to those in need rather than tying up our resources in unnecessary church assets. Find out for yourself how to stand firm in your freedom and enjoy being generous!

This newly revised version expands the original by 50%.

Available from
Emmaus Road Publishing
PO Box 38 823 Howick, Auckland 2014 New Zealand
www.emmausroad.org.nz

ISBN 978-0-9941058-1-3